Speaking Out:

Early Childhood Advocacy

Stacie G. Goffin and Joan Lombardi

National Association for the Education of Young Children
Washington, D.C.

This book is dedicated to the many advocates across the country who are taking the time to speak out for young children, families, and the early childhood profession; and to those of you who will join them along the way.

Photo credits: Shulamit Gehlfuss, cover; Cleo Freelance Photo, vi; Jeffrey High Image Productions, 20; Francis Wardle, 30; Elisabeth Nichols, 64; Anita Lynn Miller, 82.

National Association for the Education of Young Children
1509 16th St., N.W.
Washington, DC 20036-1426
202-232-8777 or 800-424-2460

The National Association for the Education of Young Children (NAEYC) attempts through its publications program to provide a forum for discussion of major issues and ideas in our field. We hope to provoke thought and promote professional growth. The views expressed or implied are not necessarily those of the Association. NAEYC wishes to thank the authors, who donated much time and effort to develop this book as a contribution to our profession.

Library of Congress Catalog Card Number: 88-062479
ISBN 0-935989-19-6
NAEYC #270

Design and production: Jack Zibulsky

Printed in the United States of America

Contents

Christ's Church Nursery School
59 Church Road
Easton, CT 06612

Acknowledgments

The texture of this book is based on the stories of many of our nation's early childhood advocates. We are particularly grateful to the following people who so willingly shared their experiences and insights with us:

Nancy DeProsse, Boston, MA	Patty Meritt, Fairbanks, AK
Andrea Fishman, Overland Park, KS	Bitsy Miller, Hattiesburg, MS
Marcia Fochler, Lafayette, CA	Kathy Modigliani, Ann Arbor, MI
Dan Gartrell, Bemidji, MN	Nancy Noble, Irvine, CA
John Gehan, Minneapolis, MN	Peggy Schirmer, Cambridge, MA
Cathy Grace, Hattiesburg, MS	Craig Simpson, Albuquerque, NM
Lana Hostetler, Springfield, IL	Louise Stoney, Albany, NY
Anne Hunt, Chattanooga, TN	Kathy Thornburg, Columbia, MO
Lee Lauber, Montpelier, VT	Billie Warford, Bozeman, MT

We also appreciate the efforts of Barbara Willer and Janet Brown McCracken, who helped edit this book; Polly Greenberg, who provided guidance and encouragement; Betty Jean Green, Cindi Potter, and Bryan Hutchins, who provided typing support; and the reviewers who took the time to read and comment on earlier drafts.

Finally, we would like to thank our families—including Neville, Nisha, and Michael Beharie; and Bruce and Sabra Goffin—for their kind and patient support of our work.

Preface

E arly childhood advocacy is about making changes—changes
to improve the lives of young children and their families,
and the status of those who work so hard to teach and care for
them. It is about convictions and compassion, empowerment and
energy, courage and consensus.

Advocacy enables you to build upon the kind of knowledge and
commitment that you as an early childhood professional have always demonstrated in your daily work with young children and
families. This book is a call to action. It focuses on the whys and
hows of advocacy, providing strategies to help you select issues,
build support, and join with others.

Many early childhood educators are already deeply involved in
advocacy. Some of their stories appear in this book as a testament
to their efforts. Hundreds more are taking place every day: People
are speaking up about developmentally appropriate curriculum,
conducting salary surveys, writing position papers, planning public
events, talking with reporters, writing letters about legislation, dis-
tributing postcards or brochures, stuffing envelopes, sharing, caring
. . . and making a difference.

A book cannot turn you into an advocate. You must feel it, live
it, and learn from your experiences as you engage in a continuous
effort to reach new parents, new administrators, new employers,
and new legislators.

We do hope that this book can demystify advocacy and help
guide you along your first steps as you begin to see yourself as an
advocate. If you are already involved in advocacy, we hope you can
use this book as you encourage others to join you.

It is time for us to speak out on what we know and believe.
Together we can move forward on the critical issues facing young
children, families, and the early childhood profession.

Chapter 1

What Is Advocacy?

*The entire ocean
is affected
by a pebble.*

Blaise Pascal

Why early childhood advocates are needed

The political process, in both the public and private sectors, directly impacts the lives of children. Children, however, lack access to the political process. If their needs were being met, this would be a small matter, but the fact is that in the United States children's needs are going unmet in many ways.

The number of young children from low-income families is rising, and these children are often placed at developmental risk. There is an increasing number of children from all socioeconomic levels who need safe and growth-promoting child care environments. At the same time, it is becoming more difficult to attract and retain qualified caregivers.

Children, therefore, are dependent upon adults (who do have political access) to speak for them, to make their needs visible, and to take part in the political process. Children need us to vote, to lobby, to inform, and to speak out on their behalf. As early childhood educators, in partnership with parents and other concerned adults, we have the power to create change. If we do not assume this responsibility, other groups competing for the same resources will be heard instead, and children's needs will remain unmet.

Adults who assume this responsibility enter the arena of early childhood advocacy. Early childhood advocacy, fundamentally, means standing up for children and their needs. "It is an attitude,

1

a process you go through, and all the steps along the way that bring about changes to help children grow and develop fully" (Beck, 1979, p. 12).

We are teachers, program directors, teacher educators, and related professionals. We experience either directly or indirectly the personal stories behind the statistics. Our professional knowledge enables us to express the relationship between children's experiences and their growth and development. Our relationships with parents create the opportunity to release parents' power on behalf of their own as well as other children (Goffin, 1988), and our connections with the community place us in a unique position to inform others about the needs of children and families.

Consequently, advocacy on behalf of children needs to become a part of our professional—and even ethical—responsibilities. Early childhood educators can serve as models of advocacy for those still unaware that the interests of children and society are mutually supportive. Advocacy is a critical vehicle for actualizing our commitment to children. Our caring cannot be restricted to our classrooms or offices if we truly want to improve the lives of children.

How we can contribute to the decision-making process

A first step in becoming an early childhood advocate is to understand the importance of advocacy, to grasp how public and private policies affect children's lives, and to accept that children need a strong voice to ensure that their environments are conducive to development. The advocate's basic question is: "What can I do to ensure adequate attention to children's needs by policymakers, elected officials, administrators, schools, businesses, and other groups?" Answering this question, however, requires advocates to take a second step—a commitment to action.

Advocacy efforts try to improve the circumstances of children's lives so they get what they need to grow to their full potential. Early childhood educators are especially well informed on this issue from both theory and practice. Early childhood advocates commit themselves to sharing this knowledge with others. They act on what they know: They move beyond good intentions and take action. Advocates overcome the fear of becoming involved and move beyond assumptions that imply children's problems are not a collective responsibility. They take the critical, transforming step between concern and action.

We *are* our governments. "That we grant every citizen the opportunity to participate in the political process is a powerful statement about the worth and dignity of each citizen from the highest to the lowest" (Kelman, 1987, p. 23). The choices our governments (and private businesses and organizations) make reflect our social values. We exercise our rights as citizens and our responsibilities as early childhood professionals when we contribute to the public debate. As early childhood educators, we expand our commitment to children, families, and our profession when we act on our beliefs and share our knowledge with others. Early childhood educators can uniquely contribute to advocacy in six ways.

Contribution #1: Sharing our knowledge

Our beliefs and knowledge are grounded in a specialized body of knowledge about child development, the practice of early childhood education, and relationships with parents. Therefore, we can make important contributions to policy debates about the developmental needs of children and the characteristics of safe and nurturing early childhood environments. This is our professional knowledge base. We need to assume responsibility for sharing these understandings with parents, policymakers, and other decision makers. We can help decision makers focus on the role of policy in enhancing children's development. In these ways, our advocacy efforts can become a catalyst for change.

Contribution #2: Sharing our professional experiences

We work with children and their families daily. We experience firsthand the impact of changing circumstances—such as unemployment, lack of child care, inappropriate curricula, and conflicts between work and family—before decision makers are informed that these issues are "new trends." When children and families in our programs receive services from public and private agencies, we are firsthand observers and monitors of whether children's needs are being met. As a result, we have the opportunity—and a professional responsibility—to share the personal stories that give meaning to group statistics. Without divulging confidential information, we can describe how policies affect children and families.

Personal experiences help us become more persuasive. According to Kelman (1987), the power of persuasion is the most underrated political resource. Stories, rather than statistics, often stimulate public policymaking. "Human interest anecdotes and concrete examples of how programs really work (or don't work) . . . are among the most influential starting points for public policy" (Phillips, in press). We live these stories in our day-to-day work with children and families.

Contribution #3: Redefining the "bottom line" for children

The debate about programs for young children is enmeshed in other policy issues such as welfare, job training, and teenage pregnancy. Funding for children's programs is often seen as an investment directed toward children's future productivity. Strategically, joining children's issues with broader political issues and social concerns is an effective political technique. These strategies can expand our base of support and help frame children's issues in ways consistent with many of society's accepted values.

Our unique perspectives on children, however, also enable us to speak out for children's inherent "worth." We know that childhood is a meaningful time for development in its own right. If policies for children and families are made solely on the basis of "return on investment," children will suffer when investors seek a higher return or decide to pull out of the "market." Early childhood educators must remember that these investment strategies are means to achieve a desired end. They must not become so effective that they undermine the "bottom line" of early childhood advocacy— encouraging policies that promote children's development.

Contribution #4: Standing up for our profession

We are living the growing pains of an emerging profession. We know how important our jobs are to children and their families. Therefore, we must simultaneously speak out on behalf of caregiving and early childhood education as a profession and for the special expertise needed to be a professional.

Many people are unaware that early childhood education has a distinctive, professional knowledge base that helps inform our practice. We know that the quality of early childhood programs depends upon the training and compensation of the staff providing the care and education. Early educators live the impact of low

4

wages, high staff turnover, burnout, and inadequately trained staff and administrators. We are obligated to share these stories, too.

Advocacy efforts on behalf of our profession are most effective when we emphasize the benefits of our work for children and families. We must begin to exercise our power to speak out on issues that affect our profession.

Contribution #5: Activating parental power

Our daily interactions with parents provide innumerable opportunities for parents and early childhood educators to recognize their common concerns and goals for children's well being. We have a unique opportunity to help parents recognize their power as children's primary advocates—for both their own and other's children.

Parents can be especially effective advocates because their vested interest is in their children. Parents represent a critical consumer voice. By activating parental power, we can dramatically expand the constituency speaking out for children.

Contribution #6: Expanding the constituency for children

Early childhood educators have important linkages with public school administrators and teachers, health care providers, religious organizations, and many other professional and volunteer groups. These interactions provide natural opportunities to inform others about the developmental needs of children, appropriate teaching practices, and the supports families need to strengthen themselves. We can act as catalysts to help others understand children's needs as our collective responsibility and our shared future.

Targets for advocacy

Early childhood educators can become involved in three areas of advocacy:

- public policy advocacy
- private-sector advocacy
- personal advocacy

Each area requires specialized knowledge and skills and a commitment to positive change.

Public policy advocacy

Public policy advocates attempt to challenge and reform public systems that affect children and families to change the broad developmental context for children's growth. This area of advocacy is directed toward the legislative, administrative, and budgetary processes. Public policy advocates try to change policies, practices, laws, and budgetary restraints to make them more responsive to children's needs.

Public policy advocacy involves all three levels of government—local, state, and federal—and can take the form of case, administrative, legislative, or class advocacy. Although all four types share the common focus of trying to change public systems for children, they vary in the target of their efforts.

Case advocacy involves efforts to secure appropriate services from a public agency for a particular child. Because of its focus on a single child, case advocacy, although very important by itself, may have limited potential for changing policies and services that affect a larger number of children (Bing & Richart, 1987).

Administrative advocacy is directed toward regulations and guidelines, program implementation, and the staff of governmental agencies. Effective administrative advocacy demands in-depth knowledge of how an agency operates and access to people who can help resolve particular issues.

Legislative advocacy involves efforts to assure that our laws protect and serve the best interests of children. Advocates in this arena identify needed legislation, evaluate proposed or existing legislation, and develop support or opposition to proposed legislative changes.

Class advocacy focuses on the needs of a large group (a class) of children and frequently involves the courts as agents of change on behalf of children. Advocates use litigation when they think chil-dren's constitutional rights have been denied. The successful litigation on behalf of children with disabilities that forced Congress to pass what is commonly known as the mainstreaming law is an example of class action litigation. The Supreme Court extended the concept of civil rights to children with disabilities, resulting in extensive new federal legislation and dramatic changes in the public school system.

Private sector advocacy

Private organizations, businesses, and institutions also set policies that affect children's growth possibilities. The content of commercial learning materials, for example, influences both teacher education programs and practices in early childhood classrooms. The world of work, another example, has important consequences for the quality of family life and parents' ability to respond effectively to the demands of childrearing.

Private sector policymaking, like public policy, involves collective decision making. Therefore, its policy process is also political. It lends itself to the same areas of advocacy described under public policy advocacy. Private-sector advocacy targets changing private (versus public) policies and practices. Therefore, the scope of its impact is usually limited to the group's constituency. Otherwise, private-sector advocacy parallels public policy advocacy and its strategies.

Personal advocacy

There are many other opportunities for early childhood educators to speak out on issues that affect young children, families, and the profession. Although sometimes these actions can lead to changes in public and private policies, they are more personal efforts, such as supporting children and families in need, raising awareness about early childhood issues with neighbors and friends, or speaking up about a school practice that needs improvement (Goffin, 1987, 1988).

Personal advocacy takes advantage of the opportunities we have to use our expertise on behalf of children and families. For example, a child care director spoke to architects and a church committee about the importance of low windows in children's classrooms—despite her uncomfortable feelings of "exceeding her proper limits." This director overcame her discomfort and anxiety and spoke out for more light and an aesthetically pleasing environment for children. Her personal advocacy efforts resulted in differently designed, more appropriate classrooms for children.

In another community, when four people (a family day care provider, a minister, a school board member, and a center director who needed space for after-school care) recognized the need for school-age child care, they organized themselves and presented their needs to a local parish. The parish agreed to supply office space, phone, and office services. Within a year, its program was serving more than 60 school-age children in 12 family day care homes (Freeman, 1986).

* * * * *

All three areas of advocacy differ from direct services to children and families. In our public policy, private-sector, and personal advocacy efforts, we go beyond the educational responsibilities of our jobs; we reach beyond teaching and caring for children and their parents. As early childhood advocates, we speak up and reach out and try to change the circumstances of children's lives. Advocacy is a necessary component of an expanded vision of the early childhood educator's role.

Understanding how public policies make a difference

Public policies help define, in significant ways, the context in which large numbers of children and their families live. Although policies made in Washington, in state capitals, and in city halls may seem far removed from our daily lives, the problems policymakers confront are the problems we are living. The solutions they contemplate become the programs and practices we implement.

Public policies represent agreements by our governments that they will perform in certain expected ways (Morgan, 1983). Public policies for children and families, therefore, are decisions that influence *our* lives and *our* work with young children. We can help others to understand the circumstances of childhood and family life and present solutions to policymakers that will enable families and early childhood educators to take better care of children.

Public policy advocates need to be knowledgeable about how public policy is made and the circumstances that influence policy decisions. Public policies are created because policymakers (legislators, public administrators) are convinced that a problem exists and that the government has responsibility to help resolve it.

A key to developing a commitment to advocacy is understanding the pervasive influence of public policies—or their absence—on children and their families. A caring advocate once remarked, "The push for advocacy comes from personal commitment to children, not an interest in politics or policy." An interest in politics or policy, however, is an expansion of our commitment to children and can significantly improve the circumstances of their lives.

The term *policy* sounds legal and abstract, far removed from our daily lives. But, in actuality, policies are plans of action. They are decisions about goals and objectives, details on how to make the desired changes, and analyses of what resources are available or needed to achieve success.

Public policies are the result of a broad-based consensus about problems and solutions. Numerous variables contribute to the ease or difficulty of achieving consensus: public opinion, political climate, participants' political skills, the personalities and vested interests of key policymakers, budget parameters, structure of existing policies, and many other factors (Hayes, 1982). The process of policymaking—of creating consensus—is therefore often intense, tumultuous, and challenging (Hayes, 1982; Kelman, 1987; Phillips, in press).

We contribute to the policy process by trying to improve conditions for children, but we do not all agree on what conditions need to be changed or what policies will result in improvements. This makes the process of advocacy a problem-solving venture (Knitzer, 1976). We need to assess opinions and information about an issue and then plan strategies to create consensus about a problem's importance and to promote support for appropriate solutions.

Differences in opinion mean that advocacy often involves conflict, confrontation, and negotiation, especially when there is competition for attention to different ideas. A major component of advocacy is developing strategies to persuade policymakers and others of your position on an issue.

Public policies are more than just decisions in favor of particular children's programs and services (Goffin, 1988; Kagan, 1988). As plans of action to promote children's growth, they also describe the kinds of relationships our society believes should exist among families, various levels of government, and the needs of children (see "Five Steps in the Policy Process," pp. 10–11).

Public policies help describe the social, economic, and political circumstances that create a range of choices parents, early childhood educators, and others can make for children. Public policies, in other words, are part of the environment that influence children's development (Bronfenbrenner, 1974; Bronfenbrenner & Weiss, 1983). Our advocacy efforts involve professional judgments about what these environments should include.

Five Steps in the Policy Process

Most of these five phases of the public policy process take place within the executive and legislative branches. The sequence and timing of each step depend in large part on the context of the situation. Policymaking is a dynamic process, so advocates may be involved in several of the steps at the same time as they work on solving a particular problem.

1. Identifying a problem that requires government action

Governments are more willing to become involved in a social problem when there is widespread agreement among many groups that a problem exists (Anderson, Brady, Bullock, & Stewart, 1984; Kelman, 1987). Advocates attempt to make children's problems public concerns. They help others see a problem's significance.

2. Convincing the government to accept responsibility for helping to solve the problem

Political leaders are more receptive to solving problems that they perceive as important (power and number of groups affected, public opinion), that capture their interest, and that they perceive as crises (Anderson et al., 1984; Kelman, 1987). Advocates can help create a concerned constituency and organize coalitions on behalf of children's issues to promote these perceptions.

3. Developing and adopting acceptable solutions to the problem

In our democracy, shared authority to make decisions adds to the complexity, as well as the frustrations, of policymaking, but it also increases the number of access points advocates have within the policy process (Kelman, 1987).

There can be various perspectives, reflecting different values, on how to solve a problem. Policymakers must find solutions to the problem that will be acceptable to all those participating in the process. This phase, therefore, usually involves considerable discussion and debate (Hayes, 1982; Kelman, 1987; Phillips, in press). Furthermore, this debate must produce solutions that can actually be put into practice (Anderson et al., 1984; Kelman, 1987). Advocates are needed to help inform the debate by contributing their professional knowledge, sharing their experiences with the issue, and helping to build community consensus.

4. Monitoring the government's solution to the problem

Once a new policy has been approved, advocates may feel their work is complete. But without implementation, policies have no effect. The way in which a policy is implemented determines how government is actually experienced by children and families. Advocates should monitor new programs and regulations to ensure that policies are transformed into practice and that they are implemented as intended.

5. Evaluating the program

The connection between proposed solutions to a problem and real-world outcome can never be predicted with absolute certainty (Anderson et al., 1984; Phillips, in press). This understanding helps us accept less-than-perfect solutions.

Early childhood advocates are often directly involved in implementing policies for children and families. We can personally describe their impact to policymakers. Because policies reflect preferred values, evaluation of the programs should consider not only observable results but also the outcomes desired for children and families and the role governments should play to achieve them (Haskins, 1980; Kamerman & Kahn, 1978; Kelman, 1987).

Based on Anderson, Brady, Bullock, & Stewart, 1984, and Kelman, 1987.

Traditionally, in the United States, responses to children's needs have reflected the opinion that parents have sole responsibility for rearing their children. Individuals and their families are viewed as self-sufficient and in control of their circumstances. These assumptions argue for a minimal government role in influencing the lives of children. As a result, government services have tended to be crisis-oriented and available only for specific, narrowly defined problems.

Proponents of more recent conceptualizations of children's issues argue that children's needs can best be met within and by their families *but* that society needs to assume more responsibility. Society needs to support parents in fulfilling their child-rearing responsibilities by providing, for example, safe and growth-enhancing early childhood programs. Within this framework, there are circumstances associated with children's growth that government problem solving can help improve. Children's well-being is considered a legitimate objective for government activity.

These differing beliefs about the appropriate relationship between government and families strongly influence the political context of policymaking. They affect what policymakers consider to be problems for government and which solutions they investigate. Yet, this is a time of dramatic social change characterized by an increasing number of employed mothers, single-parent families, impoverished children, and concern that the near future will have fewer workers with fewer skills. These demographic changes are driving early childhood education and forcing policymakers to reexamine the relationship between families and governments and the ways early childhood programs can support families and children.

Furthermore, the quality of early childhood programs is dependent upon the caliber of those who care for children. The status of early childhood educators is a leading indicator of society's esteem for children and has a significant impact on children's care and education. These links help explain why advocacy for children and their families is inseparable from advocacy on behalf of our profession. Promoting children's growth requires policies and practices that also provide opportunities, status, and resources for those caring for children (Bronfenbrenner & Weiss, 1983; Modigliani, 1986; Whitebook, 1986).

Demographic changes are also creating widespread support for early childhood programs by parents and labor, business, and diverse community groups. Early childhood educators need to take advantage of this interest and concern to advocate on behalf of children and families.

Developing your advocacy style

There is no one way—or even a best way—to turn your commitment into action. There are many levels and types of advocacy efforts, involving various quantities of resources, such as skills, interest, and time. With experience and changing personal circumstances, advocates can experiment with involvement in different kinds of advocacy. In this way, you can learn which kinds of advocacy are most satisfying and sustain your commitment.

Finding your focus

As early childhood advocates, we each have our own interests and expertise. Each of us will choose to actualize our commitment in different ways (see Figure 1.1).

Early childhood advocates are needed to respond to individual children's needs, build and enlarge the number of people willing to support children's issues (constituency building), help create new policies, monitor program implementation, and train new advocates. We can write letters, make phone calls, nurture grassroots efforts, or network with others.

Your choices will also depend on factors such as your resources (time, in-kind support, ability to travel, access to information and external funding) and your family and job demands. With the incredible variety of ways to advocate, everyone should be able to find a way to express her or his commitment.

Of course, you may refocus your advocacy efforts many times as the personal and professional circumstances of your life change and as your confidence, skills, and interests evolve. The important point to remember is that *all* these varieties of advocacy are needed to improve the lives of children and families.

Advocacy skills

Advocacy involves knowing facts, effecting changes, and building consensus. Because of these characteristics, effective advocates need expertise in the following three areas.

Content knowledge. Advocates must be knowledgeable about their discipline, for example, after-school care, kindergarten education, or health and safety standards. We must also be capable of sharing this knowledge with others in clear, accurate, and understandable ways, through either writing or speaking. Content knowledge is critical to persuading others about children's needs (see Advocates in Action, p. 16).

Figure 1.1
Actions Early Childhood Advocates Can Take

You can choose from many courses of action once you make a commitment to become an advocate for children, their families, and your profession. Here are a few of the choices:

- Share ideas for appropriate practice with other teachers and parents (instead of just observing disapprovingly).

- Explain to administrators why dittos are inappropriate learning tools for young children (rather than using them and feeling resentful that you have to practice your profession in ways inconsistent with its knowledge base).

- Explain to parents why children learn best through play (instead of bemoaning that parents are pushing their children or giving in and teaching with inappropriate methods and materials).

- Write a letter to the editor of a newspaper or magazine to respond to an article or letter (instead of just complaining about how other people don't understand the needs of children, their families, or their caregivers).

- Write to your state or federal legislators about a pending issue and share your experiences as a way to point out needs (rather than just assuming someone else will write).

- Meet someone new who is interested in early childhood education, and ask her or him to join a professional group (see Appendix F), such as NAEYC, NBCDI, SAEC, or ACEI (instead of just wondering why the person isn't involved).

- Ask a friend to go with you to a legislator's town meeting (instead of staying home because you don't want to go alone).
- Volunteer to represent your professional group in a coalition to speak out on the educational needs of young children (instead of waiting to be asked or declining because you've never done it before).
- Agree to serve on a legislative telephone tree (rather than refusing because "my phone call won't matter anyway").
- Work and learn with others to develop a position statement on a critical issue (instead of saying "I don't really know much about this topic").
- Volunteer to speak at a school board meeting about NAEYC's position statement *Developmentally Appropriate Practice in Early Childhood Programs Serving Children From Birth Through Age 8* (Bredekamp, 1987) (instead of resigning yourself to the fact that your school system doesn't understand much about early childhood education).
- Conduct a local or state survey of salaries in early childhood programs (instead of ignoring the issue because no one has the facts).
- Persuade colleagues that it is important to work toward accreditation from NAEYC's National Academy of Early Childhood Programs (rather than assuming no one wants to improve the program).

Advocates in Action

A teacher demonstrates the value of appropriate teaching practices

Despite the trend for formal, academic kindergartens, one teacher in a rural southeastern community has been able to convince the principal and parents of the value of a developmental approach.

In her 12 years of teaching, she has established a positive relationship with the principal, who has a limited background in early childhood education. She often invites him to visit her classroom and encourages him to read to the children. She gently points out what the children are learning through play and casually shares new ideas about emerging early childhood issues with him.

When they disagree, she tries to find an appropriate moment to discuss her position in a non-threatening manner. She is careful to choose areas where change is really possible. For example, although she would prefer that the children did not have to walk in a line in the hallways, she chooses not to focus on this because it does not affect the atmosphere of her room.

Parents flock to her classroom. She invites them to volunteer and share their talents. A monthly newsletter goes home to describe the children's activities. In addition, she frequently writes notes and calls parents.

She always takes time to explain how children learn. For example, when a parent asked for more math work, she explained the math concepts children learn through graphing, cooking, and other activities. The parent was satisfied and gained a greater understanding of how young children learn.

She suggests that other teachers work for small changes at first and introduce a new approach over a period of time. She believes that people accept change best when they understand what the change means. Through lots of hard work and open communication, this teacher has demonstrated the value of her ideas and has directly improved the lives of young children and their families.

Based on an anonymous interview, January 1988

Advocacy strategies. Although not a perfect science, advocacy has identifiable skills such as organizing, involving others, using the media, and assessing the political climate. Advocates need to learn these tools of the trade. In addition, there is no *one* way to change things, so advocates need to be willing and able to use a variety of approaches. Advocacy is a way of thinking about what you do. You should always be asking yourself, "Is there an opportunity in this to speak up or take action for children?" The ability to take advantage of these opportunities requires being able to call upon a variety of advocacy strategies (see Advocates in Action, p. 18).

Interpersonal skills. Advocates need others—members of the public, decision makers, and other advocates—to achieve their goals. Interpersonal skills, such as flexibility, cooperative problem solving, ability to compromise, and reflective and respectful listening, are needed to encourage cooperation and foster relationships. Strong relationships are essential to effective advocacy. All of us are more responsive to ideas proposed by people we know and respect.

There are many ways to nurture relationships. In Iowa, child care programs "adopt" key legislators for a session. They invite legislators to lunch at their center, send them children's artwork, and take children to visit their offices (Wilkins & Blank, 1986).

Developing relationships requires that people get to know each other. This entails continued involvement and time. As you build your network of contacts, keep in mind that "integrity is our most valuable currency. . . . The advocate has only one chance to misrepresent the facts. . . . Once misled, a legislator or journalist seldom, if ever, trusts an advocate again" (Bing & Richart, 1987, p. 52).

* * * * *

Creating change can be a slow and frustrating process—especially if you deeply care about the outcomes. There is also a sense of urgency because children and families bear the burden when change is slow or fails to happen. Advocates, therefore, need to be able to keep the process in perspective and still keep caring enough to try again. You have to be careful not to let the challenges associated with advocacy (confronting "experts" and bureaucrats, the complexity of "the system") deter you from your commitment.

Committing yourself to advocacy requires learning to feel justified in asserting yourself and promoting your views—over and over again. As so well expressed by Hostetler (1981), "When I become terribly frustrated, I think of the young child who is constantly being frustrated because his care setting is less than adequate. I usually find I can deal with the frustration" (p. 7).

Advocates in Action

Early childhood professionals stand up for important principles

Over the past few years there has been a proliferation of war toys produced by the toy industry. Early childhood professionals, church groups, parents, and others concerned have begun to speak out and draw public attention to the effect of such toys on young children.

In Albuquerque, New Mexico, a group of people from the local Peace Center, including child care workers, decided to survey their local toy stores to see what types of toys were for sale. This activity helped build awareness of the growing number of war toys available in the community.

At the same time, the group developed a leaflet describing the types of toys more appropriate for young children, based on the NAEYC brochure for parents on selecting toys. The leaflet was distributed to every child care center in the city and through the resource and referral agency. Church groups have also begun distribution. In addition, advocates display war toys and distribute the leaflet at conferences to emphasize the issue's importance.

One of the child care advocates involved is both a leader in the local AEYC and a member of the board of the War Resisters League. His expertise in early childhood education allows him to be a resource to the League on this topic and provide articles and other resources that tie the issues of peace and young children together.

Based on a telephone interview with Craig Simpson, February 1988

References

Beck, R. (1979). *It's time to stand up for your children: A parent's guide to child advocacy.* Washington, DC: Children's Defense Fund.

Bing, S.R., & Richart, D.W. (1987). *Fairness is a kid's game: A background paper for child advocates.* Indianapolis: The Lilly Endowment, Inc. Available from Kentucky Youth Advocates, Inc., 2024 Woodford Pl., Louisville, KY 40205.

Bronfenbrenner, U. (1974). Developmental research, public policy and the ecology of childhood. *Child Development, 45,* 1–5.

Bronfenbrenner, U., & Weiss, H.B. (1983). Beyond policies without people: An ecological perspective on child and family policy. In E.F. Zigler, S.L. Kagan, & E. Klugman (Eds.), *Children, families and government: Perspectives on American social policy* (pp. 393–414). Cambridge, England: Cambridge University Press.

Freeman, M. (1986). *Called to act: Stories of child care advocacy in our churches.* New York: Child Advocacy Office, Division of Church and Society, National Council of the Churches in the U.S.A.

Goffin, S.G. (1989). How well do we respect the children in our care? *Childhood Education, 66*(2), 68–74.

Goffin, S.G. (1988). Putting our advocacy efforts into a new context. *Young Children, 43*(3), 52–56.

Haskins, R. (1980). A model for analyzing social policies. In R. Haskins & J.J. Gallagher (Eds.), *Care and education of young children in America: Policy, politics, and social science* (pp. 1–25). Norwood, NJ: Ablex.

Hayes, C.D. (1982). *Making policies for children: A study of the federal process.* Washington, DC: National Academy Press.

Hostetler, L. (1981). Child advocacy: Your professional responsibility? *Young Children, 36*(3), 3–8.

Kagan, S.L. (1988). Current reform in early childhood education: Are we addressing the issues? *Young Children, 43*(2), 27–32.

Kamerman, S.B., & Kahn, A.J. (Eds.). (1978). *Family policy: Government and families in fourteen countries.* New York: Columbia University Press.

Kelman, S. (1987). *Making public policy: A hopeful view of American government.* New York: Basic.

Knitzer, J.E. (1976). Child advocacy: A perspective. *American Journal of Orthopsychiatry, 46,* 200–216.

Modigliani, K. (1986). But who will take care of the children? Child care, women, and devalued labor. *Journal of Education, 168*(3), 46–69.

Morgan, G.G. (1983). Practical techniques for change. *Journal of Children in Contemporary Society, 15*(4), 91–103.

Phillips, D.A. (in press). Social policy and community psychology. In J. Rappaport & E. Seidman (Eds.), *Handbook of community psychology.* New York: Plenum.

Whitebook, M. (1986). The teacher shortage: A professional precipice. *Young Children, 41*(3), 10–11.

Wilkins, A., & Blank, H. (1986). Child care: Strategies to move the issue forward. *Young Children, 42*(1), 68–72.

Chapter 2

Identifying Your Issue and Focusing Your Response

Selecting a problem

A fter making the commitment to become an advocate, you need to target your efforts. This is the first step in the advocacy process. Because so many issues need attention, it is easy to feel overwhelmed and to question one's ability to make a difference. The only way to overcome this inertia is to *do something*.

Begin by choosing an area of personal interest and concern. The issue should be one you care enough about to commit your time and energy to it. The topic should also be one you will enjoy learning more about because advocates need to be well informed.

You may be tempted to define your issue in general terms, such as the need to improve child care, or to provide public school programs for 3- and 4-year-olds. Concerns such as these, however, are too broad for specific advocacy efforts because they do not concretely identify what changes are expected of decision makers and do not provide a clear focus for advocacy activity. These issues are obviously appropriate areas of concern, but they need to be broken down into manageable pieces for action—both for yourself and for decision makers. Advocacy efforts need to be focused on specific concerns such as teacher-child ratios, kindergarten class size, or availability of program slots for low-income families. Try asking yourself the following questions as you try to identify the problem you want to tackle (adapted from Beck, 1979, p. 25; Bing & Richart, 1987, p. 60):

- What is the problem? How many children, families, or professionals does it affect? Why is this particular problem a priority to you or your organization? Answers to these questions will help you determine an appropriate form of advocacy to address the problem.
- How harmful is the problem? Does it have serious effects on children? Can the problem be presented to the public in ways that will generate concern?
- What kinds of changes are you seeking? What are their chances of being implemented? Can you identify specific ways to bring about change? How easy (or difficult) will it be to create change(s)? What skills, resources, knowledge, time, and other factors are necessary for their implementation?
- Is anyone else working on this problem? If no one else is, why not? Who can you invite to join you? If others are already involved, how can you join their efforts? Duplication of effort is an unproductive use of time and commitment.

Gathering the facts

After you or your group have decided which problem to focus on, continue the investigation until all your questions are answered (see Advocates in Action, pp. 24–25). Depending upon the problem selected, gathering facts and becoming informed on an issue will vary in difficulty, complexity, time, and effort. It requires asking enough questions and getting enough answers to feel you have a firm grasp of the problem and some possible solutions so you can present your case in a convincing, persuasive way (Beck, 1979).

During this fact-finding process, it is extremely important to document your findings. Keep meticulous records of names, addresses, phone numbers, and statements from both individuals and organizations so you can verify facts or obtain more information easily. Gathering this information enables you to evaluate the issue critically, ask good questions, feel confident in expressing your concerns, and substantiate them with facts.

It is also important to become familiar with the opposition, even though their arguments and tactics may make you angry. Understanding their arguments (from reading their newsletters and attending their meetings) helps increase your effectiveness when responding to their concerns and formulating your response.

The following questions can help you learn more about your issue (adapted from Beck, 1979; Bing & Richart, 1987; Shur & Smith, 1980):

- Who else is affected by your concern—other children, parents, early childhood educators, public school programs? If so, how many seem to be affected? Is this a local issue? Or a state or national issue? How are others trying to handle the problem? Are any census data available to bolster your arguments?

- Do any rules, regulations, or policies affect the problem? Have any administrative, budget, or special commission reports been released on your topic? Are there priority statements or future plans that affect the problem? Have government officials issued any statements? How can you use this information to describe your problem and to formulate solutions?

- Are any organizations and/or experts interested in the same problem? What are their positions on your concerns? Are there lawyers, account-ants, auditors, or other experts who will help you interpret reports, legal papers, or budgets, for example? What information, statistics, or policy recommendations are available from national organizations such as those listed in Appendix F?

- Are there individuals or organizations who disagree with your stance or proposed solutions? What are their reasons? What strategies do they use to present their arguments?

- Whose names seem to be mentioned over and over? Who are these people, what do they do, and what do they think about the problem? If you are dealing with an organization, what is the chain of com-mand? Who is most likely to be helpful?

Answers to these questions will help sort out how your problem is perceived by others and how public and private institutions are respond-ing to it. They will also help make later decisions regarding strategies more effective.

Advocates in Action

Michigan advocates gather the facts and clearly present their case

In 1983, a small group of child care professionals in Washtenaw County, Michigan, came together to explore their mutual concerns about the quality of available child care. The group consisted of directors, teachers, resource and referral workers, and other advocates. They shared a vague fear that the quality of child care was beginning to erode and that it was further threatened by changes only beginnning to appear on the horizon. They were particularly worried about the number of good teachers and directors in the county who had recently left the field and reports from centers that they could not find qualified applicants to fill job openings.

After identifying their concerns more clearly, they realized that the prerequisite for high-quality programs was that they be able to find and keep high-quality staff members. In their experience, the salaries and working conditions in the field were critical to this ability. They knew salaries were low—but how low? They knew that many teachers and directors did not have even minimal fringe benefits. But they did not have any concrete information about salaries or working conditions, or even a description of who was providing care in the county. Because of this, they decided to do a survey to collect detailed information that they could use when talking to others about these problems.

The Working Conditions Project became an official task force of the Washtenaw County AEYC. The task force surveyed each child care center and nursery school in the county and all teaching and administrative staff members in those programs. Everyone worked hard to keep potential factions together: teachers and directors, nonprofit and for-profit

Other sources of information

Many people and publications are available to help build your case. The following are a few types of resources that can assist your effort.

Research findings. These can give an issue credibility and substance. They can recommend changes that have been demonstrated to be effective. They also help decision makers better understand social issues, focus on problems in new ways, and consider different possibilities for policy solutions (Peters, 1980; Hayes, 1982; Glass, 1987; Phillips, in press). For example, research findings about the long-

organizations, child care professionals and parents. The fluctuating group of coordinators met weekly for two years. An especially successful aspect of the project was the use of 41 trained liaisons who worked with two centers each to invite participation and administer the surveys.

Whenever the project needed help, people who cared about child care and young children donated their services. The Survey Research Center at the University of Michigan provided assistance. A design firm that sponsored on-site child care for its employees designed and printed handsome graphics and stationery and helped with some of the mailings. An NAEYC Membership Action Group (MAG) grant, the Ann Arbor Area Foundation, and the Michigan and Washtenaw AEYCs provided funding.

The results of the survey have been used extensively in presentations to parents, local policymakers, community groups, and journalists. In advocating for higher wages, advocates found that the contrasts of child care employee salaries with public school employees with similar levels of education was particularly effective. Several hundred copies of a six-page summary of findings were distributed nationally and a single-page summary was included in the Michigan AEYC conference registration packets. Reference to specific findings, especially about salaries and benefits, has appeared in several state and national publications, newsletters, and a position statement. Results and procedures are available through ERIC (ED 275415).

Based on personal correspondence with Kathy Modigliani, January 1988

term benefits of Head Start and other preschool programs have led to continued support for these programs.

Professional and advocacy organizations can be helpful in informing you about relevant research. Be careful, however, to note the circumstances of a program's success and the kinds of children and families involved so you do not overgeneralize the research and accidentally apply the results to a different kind of problem. Also, remember that research findings can be used to either affirm *or* deny potential solutions.

Figure 2.1
Excerpt From a Legislative Platform

Child Care Programs and Services

Group will support:

1. Increased affordability of licensed child care services through government funding and/or tax benefits to families
2. Supplemental funding to provide care for children of the working poor
3. Improved licensing standards that address group size, teacher/child ratio, caregiver education/training, and program criteria, including use of developmentally appropriate methods, materials, and curricula as outlined by the National Assocation for the Education of Young Children
4. Mandatory in-service training (a minimum of 24 hours per year) for directors, caregivers, family day care providers, and child care licensing representatives
5. Mandatory licensing for all child care programs
6. Use of a variety of facilities (including school buildings) for before- and after-school care

Public School Programs

Group will support:

1. The direct leadership of early childhood professionals in the development of curricula and standards for public school early childhood programs
2. Preschool and kindergarten programs taught only by teachers with educational background on the development of 3- through 5-year-olds and practical experience with 3- through 5-year-olds

Child Abuse Prevention

Group will support:

1. All child care staff to be involved in ongoing training in appropriate methods and techniques of working with young children and indicators of child maltreatment
2. All employers of day care staff to keep employment screening records (interview materials and reference checks) on all staff of child day care
3. Developing within day care rules an appeal process for when child abuse is reported in child care center/homes

Adapted from AEYC-MO 1988 legislative platform

Platforms, resolutions, and position statements. Groups sometimes structure their focus and prioritize their concerns in written form.

Platforms are frequently associated with political campaigns, and advocates can work to get information about their issue included in a party's platform. But organizations and groups also use platform statements or legislative agendas to present preferred solutions to social problems. Most such platforms are lists of statements grouped into categories such as child care and early childhood education, health, and public school programs (see Figure 2.1). Advocates use platform statements to demonstrate broad support for their issues and proposed solutions. Platforms also identify groups that may be willing to work on your issue.

Resolutions are formal statements of a group's concern and commitment to resolve an issue in a particular way. They are usually less than one page in length and include the group's rationale and statements of resolve or desired action. You can use resolutions, like platforms, to demonstrate a group's support for your issue, and as a resource for information and coalition building.

Position statements are most frequently developed by professional organizations, special task forces, or commissions. These documents go beyond reports because they thoroughly examine an issue and, based upon critical analysis of the information, develop conclusions and recommendations for action.

Position statements can help advocates learn more about their issue. Helping draft such a statement provides an opportunity to clarify your thinking and develop your expertise on the issue.

Focusing your response

Support for an issue, as well as its success or failure with policymakers, depends not only on its merits, but also on how the issue is focused (Wilkins & Blank, 1986). Focusing your issue helps you define it for yourself and for other advocates, provides a consistent theme for your advocacy efforts, and provides a way for parents, school superintendents, legislators, and any others involved to understand and support your issue.

The process begins by *assessing the current political climate* in your community or state (Wilkins & Blank, 1986; Bing & Richart, 1987; Kelman, 1987). Ask yourself, How can the issue be linked to current values and concerns to increase the likelihood that my thinking—or that of my group—will be accepted? This requires connecting your issue with other social, economic, and/or political circumstances.

In Ohio and North Carolina, for example, when there was media attention on child abuse, advocates seized the opportunity to target improvements in those states' child care licensing laws. In Virginia, advocates built on the state's emphasis on rapid economic expansion and accompanying employment opportunities by focusing on the need for child care assistance for low-income working families as an economic issue (Wilkins & Blank, 1986).

An issue should be kept as simple and focused as possible—without being misleading. *Fact sheets and reports* are effective ways to highlight the major issues and provide supporting data both for your group and for others who are less informed.

These documents can range from one-page fact sheets (that identify the issue, document your stance, and list major recommendations) to brochures or printed reports with glossy covers.

The length and detail of the documents will depend upon the topic, the knowledge base of those you are trying to convince, and the advocates' resources. Extensive reports obviously require more time, expense, and expertise. You also need to consider the views and needs of your readers. Their different perspective and motivations need to be reflected in the way you frame your materials (Wilkins & Blank, 1986; Kelman, 1987; Phillips, in press).

Regardless of length, reports and fact sheets should be clearly written, attractively organized, and, if possible, professionally presented. At the very least, use typewritten materials. Be sure to include the name and telephone number of a person who can provide further information.

Getting ready for action

After selecting, investigating, and organizing your area of concern, the next step is to determine *how* to share your knowledge. What advocacy strategies will best get your message to others? You can ask yourself these questions as you start to decide what actions to take:

● What is your purpose? What specific outcomes(s) do you hope to accomplish? (Do you want public school principals to become more aware of appropriate teaching and learning in kindergarten? Do you want parents to be better informed about the connection between early childhood educators' salaries and the quality of care and education children receive? Do you want legislators to improve state child care licensing regulations?) Different advocacy strategies are appropriate for achieving different purposes.

- Who can make the decision to create your proposed change(s)? Where will the changes be considered (private or public sector)? At what level (local, state, national)? Answers to these questions will help you tailor information and stategies to fit the need of the recipients.
- What is your personal advocacy style? What do you enjoy doing? What do you have the time and resources to accomplish?
- Will you be advocating as an individual or joining with others? Individual and group advocacy efforts succeed with different strategies, depending on how many people will be contributing and what their individual styles are. Both individual and group advocacy efforts are needed to enhance the well-being of children and their families.

No one strategy will always work. Each advocacy experience is different because the people and issues involved vary. Advocates must be prepared to use a variety of techniques and to be persistent. Change takes time. "Staying power is absolutely necessary to child power" (Knitzer, 1976, p. 207).

References

Beck, R. (1979). *It's time to stand up for your children: A parent's guide to child advocacy.* Washington, DC: Children's Defense Fund.

Bing, S.R., & Richart, D.W. (1987). *Fairness is a kid's game: A background paper for child advocates.* Indianapolis: The Lilly Endowment, Inc. Available from Kentucky Youth Advocates, Inc., 2024 Woodford Pl., Louisville, KY 40205.

Glass, G.V. (1987). What works: Politics and research. *Educational Researcher, 16*(3), 5–10.

Hayes, C.D. (1982). *Making policies for children: A study of the federal process.* Washington, DC: National Academy Press.

Kelman, S. (1987). *Making public policy: A hopeful view of American government.* New York: Basic.

Knitzer, J.E. (1976). Child advocacy: A perspective. *American Journal of Orthopsychiatry, 46,* 200–216.

Peters, D.L. (1980). Social science and social policy and the care of young children: Head Start and after. *Journal of Applied Developmental Psychology, 1*(1), 7–27.

Phillips, D.A. (in press). Social policy and community psychology. In J. Rappaport & E. Seidman (Eds.), *Handbook of community psychology.* New York: Plenum.

Shur, J.L. & Smith, P.V. (1980). *Where do you look? Whom do you ask? How do you know?* Washington, DC: Children's Defense Fund.

Wilkins, A., & Blank, H. (1986). Child care: Strategies to move the issue forward. *Young Children, 42*(1), 68–72.

Chapter 3

Building Support for Your Concern

> A preschool teacher sends a copy of the NAEYC Position Statement on Developmentally Appropriate Practice to his local licensing official.
>
> A child care director invites her state delegate to tour her recently accredited center and calls the local newspaper to cover the event.
>
> A kindergarten teacher writes to a television network to voice concern about violent cartoons.
>
> A college instructor testifies at a public hearing about how difficult it is to attract new students to the early childhood field due to low salaries, even though there are many jobs open for trained teachers.
>
> The director of a child care resource and referral agency speaks to the local chamber of commerce about child care options for working parents.

Early childhood professionals have firsthand experience with issues facing young children and families. No matter what your role, the expertise you have developed over the years provides a wealth of information to share with decision makers and the general public. You can build support for your issue by sharing your expertise with parents, public officials, employers, and the media.

Encouraging parents to speak out

Early childhood education has a long tradition of parent involvement—it is a cornerstone of our programs. We know that parent-child relationships are intense and enduring, so parents are most often the best advocates for their own children. They also may grow as advocates for *all* children as they recognize the impact young children's experiences can have not only on their families but on all of society.

Decision makers see parents as consumers of services for their children, so parents' opinions are crucial. Our role is to show parents how much their voice counts so they can speak out as effectively as possible. Our partnership with families enables us to support parents' roles, build their capacity as decision makers for children, model effective advocacy strategies, and link parents with other resources.

Our relationships with parents will be more supportive if we believe in and act on these assumptions (Goffin & Caccamo, 1986):

- Most parents wish to be good parents.
- Parenting is a challenging job. It is demanding, time consuming, and never ending.
- Childrearing is a highly personal endeavor.
- Parents bring skills, knowledge, and individual differences to parenting.

We can encourage parents to make the best decision for children when we respect their choices and offer new perspectives on childrearing. Parental awareness is enhanced whenever we talk about developmentally appropriate practice or other relevant topics, or when we share information on their child's daily activities.

Furthermore, we can expand parents' abilities and self-confidence to be decision makers (first in the program, then more widely in the community) by providing opportunities for them to express opinions that lead to changes. Including parents on committees that plan the curriculum, hire staff, and develop the budget tells them that you value their opinions and roles as decision makers.

You can serve as a model advocate to parents by sharing your own experiences. Keep parents informed about what you are doing and encourage them to take part in the political process. Talk about legislation and emerging issues with parents, in groups or through newsletters. Give them an opportunity to express their opinions and tell their stories in letters or testimony. By respecting the contributions of parents, we can fine tune the crucial consumer voice that moves children's and family issues forward.

Be cautious, however, not to overwhelm parents by demanding their political involvement. Parents as well as colleagues usually need to be nurtured as advocates. This story demonstrates how an advocate can support parent growth in this direction:

> A mother in Vermont quit her job because she was unhappy with her child's overcrowded family day care home, one of the only affordable child care options available in her community. When hearings were scheduled in the state to consider increasing the number of children in family day care homes, an early childhood advocate encouraged the mother to testify. With little experience in the political process, the mother was naturally hesitant to come forward and tell her story. She did agree, however, to attend the hearings. After listening to the testimony of others, she told the advocate, "I could have done it." (L. Lauber, personal communication, January 1988)

Although the parent was not ready to testify, she learned about the political process by attending this hearing. By watching other people voice similar concerns, she gained the confidence that could enable her to speak out in the future.

As early childhood advocates, we also need to share information about community resources to support families, and to help parents network with each other. These ties break down the sense of isolation so common in our mobile, fragmented society and establish a foundation for sharing and doing something about common concerns.

For more information about parents as advocates, see *It's Time To Stand Up for Your Children* (Beck, 1979) and *Parent to Parent* (Pizzo, 1983).

Informing public officials

Decision makers need to hear from you to stay informed about the issues that you confront daily. Both elected and appointed officials must respond to a wide variety of issues. Because children are a voiceless and invisible constituency (Allen, 1983), it is our professional responsibility to make sure problems facing children, families, and early childhood staff are addressed.

Legislators

Legislators generally make laws, appropriate funds, monitor government activities, investigate problems, respond to constituent concerns, and to some degree educate citizens about the issues.

Your legislators most likely include two U.S. senators and one U.S. representative (all three represent you in Washington, D.C.), one state senator and one state delegate (both represent you in your state capital), and a host of local town, city, and/or county council members.

Local, state, and federal legislative districts vary and overlap to some degree. On the other hand, you may live and work in different jurisdictions. If you do, and are representing your program, you can be active in the district in which you work. If you are speaking as a constituent, contact legislators from your home district.

U.S. senators and representatives work full-time in their positions, but state and local legislators often work part-time as elected officials and hold other jobs in the community. Federal and state legislators often have home offices in their districts as well as offices in the capital. Ask your local League of Women Voters or reference librarian for contact information.

Most legislators have assistants to help them sort through the complexity and number of issues. Call your legislator's office to find out the names and responsibilities of legislative staff, what issues the legislator is interested in, and what committees she or he serves on.

In addition, find out how your legislator has voted on key issues related to children. The Children's Defense Fund (see Appendix G) regularly compiles information on the voting records of members of the U.S. Congress on children's issues.

It also may be useful to know some personal information about your legislator. Does she or he have children? Are any in child care or preschool? What about grandchildren? Do any members of the family work in education? Such information, along with an understanding of the political climate, will help guide you in your advocacy efforts (Wilkins & Blank, 1986).

Once you identify the key people, begin a get-acquainted campaign (Hostetler, 1983). You may have 5 or 10 elected officials who represent you (federal, state, and local), so select one or two at a time to get to know. Be nonpartisan in whom you contact first, and avoid the temptation to focus only on those who have already demonstrated support for children's issues. Remember, your goal as an advocate is to provide information and change opinion.

The people you focus on will shift as issues and legislative proposals change. For example, in 1981, when human service programs were cut at the federal level, advocates turned their attention to state legislators. In 1988, when important early childhood legislation was introduced in Congress, U.S. senators and representatives were key figures.

Hostetler (1983) suggests that a good way to begin to get acquainted with elected officials is to send them a congratulatory letter upon their election or a simple letter of introduction. In either case, make your letter straightforward, precise, and positive. Provide basic facts about yourself and your work. You may want to include brief articles, fact sheets, or other relevant information.

Establishing a relationship takes continual contact. Perhaps you can put your legislator on a mailing list for your program's or NAEYC Affiliate Group's newsletter. When you come across some important information, forward it with a note: "Just wanted to let you know what important activities the children and families in your district are involved in." By doing so, you develop legislators' awareness of children's programs and issues. Even if they never thoroughly read the material, they know you are out there working with the families they represent.

Another way to keep in touch is to send "Dear Legislator" letters every few months. You receive letters about critical legislation as a constituent, so you can keep legislators informed about needs and issues you encounter. See Appendix C about the types of information you can share with your legislators. You may want to attach a note to printed materials, such as "Remember the _____ bill in your upcoming session," to reinforce your efforts with each legislator in the district.

One of the best ways to become acquainted with decision makers is to invite them to visit a high-quality program for young children. Arrange a tour just before the legislative session begins, when the legislator is home on recess, or when the legislator is campaigning in your district (see "When You Invite a Legislator to a Program," p. 36).

As you establish a relationship with legislators and their staffs, they will come to rely on you as a community expert on early childhood issues. Your opinion will then have more significance when decisions are made.

When You Invite a Legislator to a Program

- *Telephone if time is short, or send a letter of invitation* on official stationery, explaining the event. Provide options for dates and times so the visit fits into the legislator's schedule.

- Suggest inviting the local newspaper or television station. The legislator's staff may assist in getting *press coverage*. Write a short press release describing the event. Work with the legislator's office to develop the material.

- *Outline points you want to make* when you meet. Determine what roles staff, parents, and board members will have in these discussions. Prepare short fact sheets to summarize your program and key points. Put them in a packet for the legislator and staff.

- *Talk about the visit in advance* with children, parents, and staff. Children should keep to their normal routine rather than perform for the legislator.

- *Be positive and gracious to the legislator.* Allow plenty of opportunities for her or him to ask questions and meet parents and children.

- *Follow up with a thank-you letter* to the legislator and staff.

Administrators

The executive branch of government—at the federal, state, or local level—administers the agencies that implement laws passed by the legislature.

At the federal level, the chief executive is the president. The president's cabinet is composed of appointed secretaries of the major departments (see Appendix B). Family and children's programs are administered by a variety of agencies within several departments including Health and Human Services, Education, Agriculture, Justice, and Labor. These agencies are not always required to coordinate programs with each other.

Your state executive branch includes your governor and several appointees, somewhat similar to the federal structure. City and county governments, on the other hand, may have elected or appointed executives. Several state and local agencies are responsible for programs for children and families, and the degree of coordination among them varies. Some states have special agencies or offices to promote the interests of children. They may fund and ad-

36

minister programs or just report on and coordinate services.

Administrative officials who plan and monitor programs, such as licensing staff or early childhood specialists from various agencies, are usually informed about the issues we face. Many of them have had experience in the field. Nevertheless, they still rely on our expertise to keep them informed about how policy decisions affect programs and families and to provide ideas for future plans.

Elected and appointed administrators, such as the governor or mayor, are less likely to be informed on early childhood issues. You can become aquainted with and provide information to these key administrators just as you do with legislators by introducing yourself, inviting them to visit a good program, and writing and calling them in response to specific issues.

Board, council, and commission members

A wide variety of boards, councils, commissions, and citizens' advisory groups affect early childhood concerns. Members may be elected or appointed to these positions, and their expertise in the field varies. Some groups set policies; others are advisory. These groups include state and local school boards, boards or advisory councils to administrative agencies and/or legislatures, and appointed study commissions (such as a Superintendent's Task Force on Early Childhood Education).

You can get to know the key players in these groups by reading your newspaper, attending public hearings, and obtaining copies of their reports. Contact the office that works with the group to obtain a list of all group members. For example, obtain your state school board member list from your state's education agency.

Your influence with these groups can affect both legislative and administrative decisions. Often, once you have "gained the ear" of one member, you can have your opinions expressed to the group through this contact. Your attendance and testimony at the hearings, and responses to the groups' reports, are crucial. Citing their reports in fact sheets and letters to legislators and administrators can help build momentum for your issue.

Responding to legislation

When you get to know decision makers and build awareness of early childhood issues, you set the stage for you or your group to respond to, or propose, specific legislation to address these issues. Attempting to influence legislation at the local, state, or federal level is called *lobbying*. Although the term may sound intimidating, "it is nothing more than getting the right information to the right person at the right time" (Tyler-Wilkins & Blank, 1987, p. 75).

Lobbying includes

- Contacting legislators, their staff, or government employees to encourage them to propose, support, oppose, or otherwise influence legislation;
- Trying to get the public to share your views on the legislation and to take action on it; and
- Advocating for the adoption or rejection of a particular piece of legislation (Children's Defense Fund, 1983).

As a private citizen, you have every right to express your views on legislation. If you represent a nonprofit organization, within certain limits, you can still conduct lobbying activities (see Appendix D and "Advocates in Action," p. 39).

Putting it in writing

When you have established your credibility, you or your group may be asked to respond to legislation. If you are asked to respond, it is important to (1) know what is expected of you and (2) fully understand the issue at hand. First, you will need to find answers to questions such as these:

- What is this legislation all about? How will it affect young children and families in your community? (See Appendix E for other guidelines about proposed legislation.)
- Which legislators should be contacted? Why? Which legislators are on key committees?
- What will you ask the legislator to do? Cosponsor? Vote in committee? Vote on the floor? (See Appendix A about the path legislation follows.)
- When should contacts be made?
- What feedback does your group need about the legislator's response?
- What other people should be notified about your effort? Parents? Other early childhood advocates? Community groups?

Advocates in Action

Mississippi advocates help establish kindergarten in the state

Over the past 10 years, members of the Mississippi Association for Children Under Six (MACUS) have had an interesting firsthand learning experience in becoming politically involved. In its infancy, MACUS's political involvement focused on inviting legislators and other state officials to MACUS public policy meetings to inform them about the organization's concerns. As MACUS grew in its political involvement, it ventured into the legislators' territory—their offices and legislative committee meetings at the state capital.

Prior to the 1982 Mississippi Education Reform Act, there was no state law mandating statewide, state-funded kindergarten in public schools. In the late 1970s and early 1980s, a network of 30 MACUS members realized that the organization could do a great deal to promote the idea of public kindergarten and its importance to the children of Mississippi and to the state's future.

The MACUS Executive Board budgeted funds for network members' travel expenses. With this support, network members became part of a speaking circuit. By calling the program chairman or the presidents of numerous local groups, network members, and other groups across the state, MACUS took the idea of statewide public kindergarten to the people.

The governor also generated grassroots support for passage of the bill when he spoke at regional rallies across the state about education and economic conditions. In 1982, he called a special session of the legislature and the comprehensive Mississippi Education Reform Act was passed.

Once the act was passed, advocates started work to assure funding. In 1986, when key legislators began to withdraw their support for funding, MACUS activated a telephone tree. The Public Policy Chair called the affiliate presidents and several other key network members in the state. Each of those people called about 10 other MACUS members and each of those called 10 others until 400 members had been alerted. Members called their local legislators. If the legislator was a supporter of the legislation, MACUS members asked him or her to talk with the legislators who had withdrawn their support. All this effort worked—when the vote was called, the legislation for funding kindergarten passed.

Based on personal correspondence with Bitsy Miller and Cathy Grace, 1988

39

When Writing to Your Legislators

- *Avoid professional jargon.* Terms you use every day mean very little to them, just as legislative terms may be unfamiliar to you.
- *Avoid ranting or tear-jerking approaches.* A poignant need or a grave injustice, simply told, can have far greater impact.
- *Focus upon one issue per letter.* Keep the letter short.
- *Use real-life examples* to illustrate your point. Legislators may use grassroots stories to persuade colleagues to cosponsor a bill or to vote for or against it (see Figure 3.1). Your example may even enliven a member's speech or floor statement.
- *Check that your facts are accurate.* Use the proper form of address (see Figure 3.2, pp. 44–45). Refer to bills by name or number. Organize your arguments so they are clear and cogent.
- *Avoid form letters.* However, if you are using a form letter, paraphrase, insert a personal example, use your own handwriting, or type it yourself.
- Open and close with statements that will *establish rapport:* "I know you are concerned with the welfare of young children and will take appropriate action on this issue."
- *Show your strength.* Mention the number of families you serve or the number of professionals you represent.
- *Write (or call) more than once.* Your input is critical at three stages:

Once you have this information, you will be in a better position to act. When your professional organization or some other group asks you to respond, try to find the time to do it. Your letter makes a difference because it represents *your voice* on an issue (see "When Writing to Your Legislators," above).

Sometimes special group mail-in campaigns help keep an issue alive in the legislature or catch the attention of legislative staff. In Illinois, the state AEYC printed 3,000 red postcards. Early childhood advocates sent the card to a particular senator to encourage his support of specific legislation. The cards read, "Show the families of Illinois that your heart is with them on Valentine's Day! Become a cosponsor of S. 1885, the Act for Better Child Care" (L. Hostetler, personal communication, January 1988).

1. Initially, to urge your representative to cosponsor the bill;
2. Next, to encourage the committee to pass the proposed legislation and to encourage your representative to exercise pressure on the committee to pass it; and
3. Before it comes to a full vote, to urge your representative to vote for the bill.

- *Watch your timing.* If your member sits on a committee with jurisdiction over a bill, the time to make recommendations is before the committee has reported out the bill. (A bill is reported out when it is passed from the committee to the floor.) When time is running out, send telegrams or telephone your representative.

- *Ask for a response.* Include your name and address on the letter (envelopes may be thrown away).

- *Write a letter of appreciation* if your representative acts in accordance with your recommendations. Reiterate the specific, appropriate actions taken by your representative (this extends the life and focus of the issue). Let it be known you are spreading the good word in your group's newsletter or at a forthcoming meeting.

Adapted from "Children, the Congress, and You" by K. E. Allen, 1983, *Young Children, 38*(2), 71–75. Copyright 1983 by the National Association for the Education of Young Children. Adapted by permission.

Similarly, the Pennsylvania Women's Agenda developed a postcard series depicting a range of issues of concern to the group. Organizers gave parents, child care providers, and other supporters a list of names and addresses of legislators and asked each individual to write a personal message to achieve the greatest impact (Wilkins & Blank, 1987).

Sending telegrams or making phone calls

Telegrams, messages, and telephone calls may be more effective than letters when immediate action is required. Legislators often are required to make fast decisions—so you need to be prepared to act quickly.

Figure 3.1
Example of a Letter From an Individual to a Legislator

Dear Representative:

I feel a need to write to you because I believe it is important for you to understand the position of an early childhood educator.

Presently, early childhood educators need your help. Please support the Act for Better Child Care. This bill supports salary raises for dedicated employees and would furnish money to train staff, which would, in turn, enhance their knowledge and self-respect. This would develop professionalism, which would greatly increase the quality of care our children need and deserve.

I am a director of a not-for-profit child development center and am responsible for 150 children, 125 families, and 30 staff members. I have worked at this center for 6 1/2 years and have been the director for 3 1/2 of those years.

In May 1988, I will have my master's degree in early childhood education. I direct a very good center, licensed by the state of Kansas. I work from 40 to 60 hours a week, twelve months a year. I also work in the late evenings as well as the very early mornings, for I need to locate substitutes when staff become ill or need to be absent for family reasons on short notice. I attend evening meetings as well on a periodic basis, i.e., parent committee meetings, board meetings, and conferences with parents.

As an early childhood educator, I wear many hats. I am a teacher, social worker, psychologist, nurse, doctor, parent, business manager, bookkeeper, cook, janitor, mover, and referee—just to name a few. I am paid approximately _____ per hour, based on a

40-hour week with no overtime. I am 30 years old, single, and live in a small apartment. I live paycheck to paycheck. I am paying off two student loans besides having responsibility for my monthly living expenses. Rarely do I have enough money left over to fill my car with gas or buy groceries. I am grateful each day that I do not have a family to support.

Aside from this, I love what I do; I am good at what I do; I am proud of my child development center and of the job I do. I am working in a field that really suits me and uses my talents. Because of these things I remain where I am, but I am saddened when I see how the community appears to have little or no respect for my chosen profession. I feel it is unjust that I may have to give up my profession because I need to earn more money to support my basic needs. It is unfair that an athlete, celebrity, lawyer, doctor, or corporate employee receives an incredible salary and is respected by our society. Those who choose the profession of early childhood education have to beg, borrow, and "steal" respect and support from this same society. I want to stay in this profession because it is my life. I have worked very hard pursuing quality child care.

I write this letter on behalf of other directors and the devoted teachers who have chosen this field out of pure dedication to the young children of our society. We ask you to support the Act for Better Child Care.

Sincerely,

Submitted by Andrea Fishman, The Child Development Center, Jewish Community Center of Greater Kansas City

Figure 3.2
Forms of Salutation Used When Writing to Public Officials

Federal officials

The President
The President of the United States
The White House
Washington, DC 20500

Dear Mr. President:

U.S. senator
The Honorable (full name)
U.S. Senate
Washington, DC 20510

Dear Senator (last name):

U.S. representative
The Honorable (full name)
U.S. House of Representatives
Washington, DC 20515

Dear Congressman/Congresswoman (last name):

State officials

Governor
The Honorable (full name)
Governor, State of _____
State Capitol
City, State ZIP

Dear Governor (last name):

State senator
Senator (full name)
State Capitol
City, State ZIP

Dear Senator (last name):

State representative
Representative (full name)
State Capitol
City, State ZIP

Dear Representative (last name):

Local officials

The mayor
The Honorable (full name)
City or Town Hall
City, State ZIP

Dear Mayor (last name):

Members of local councils and boards
Councilman/Councilwoman or Supervisor (full name)
City, Town, or County Seat
City, State ZIP

Dear Councilman/Councilwoman or Supervisor (last name):

Telegrams are more concrete than phone calls and faster than a letter. There are several kinds of Western Union and post office telegrams from which to choose. Telephone calls to your legislator's local office or to the capital have the advantage of being immediate and enable you to ask or answer questions (see "When Calling Your Legislator," below).

When Calling Your Legislator

- *Identify yourself.* Explain that you live in and/or represent families or early childhood professionals in the legislator's district.

- *Ask to speak to the legislator or the legislative assistant who covers children's issues.* You will often be put through to an assistant.

- *Identify the bill* of concern by name and number. Ask how the legislator expects to vote.

- *Urge a vote in favor of your position.* Provide information on how the bill will affect children, families, and early childhood professionals in the legislator's district.

- *Know your facts.* If you are asked a question you cannot answer, say that you are not sure about the point but that you will find out and get back to her or him. Be sure to locate the information and respond.

- *Follow up with a short note* to the person with whom you spoke. Emphasize your key points, ask to be kept informed about the bill's progress, and thank the staff member for attention to the issue.

Visiting your legislator

A personal visit to your legislator's office, either in the capital or at home in the district office, is an effective way to discuss pending legislation or issues of concern (see "When Visiting Your Legislator," p. 47).

You may feel intimidated on your first visit to a legislative office. Once you have done it, however, you will be encouraged by how easy it really was to talk with people who seemed interested in your issue. You may also be stirred to action by the need for more efforts on behalf of young children and their families.

As you gain experience and confidence, you can expand upon your visit by sharing your successes with others. One Arizona advo-

When Visiting Your Legislator

- *Know your legislator's record.* Find out how she or he voted on previous children's issues. If visiting a member of Congress, contact the Children's Defense Fund for its congressional voting record list for the year. If visiting a state legislator, contact a state advocacy group for more information on the legislator's record.

- *Schedule an appointment.* If your legislator is unavailable on that day, arrange to meet with the staff person who handles child and family issues. If you meet at the capital, arrange to see as many legislators as you can, allowing time to get from one office to the next between your appointments.

- *Draft an agenda.* List the early childhood issues you want to discuss. If you are going with a group, each person should play a role. One person can open the meeting, another can be the recorder, someone can keep the conversation on the agenda, and another can leave a fact sheet or other literature.

- *Arrive on time.* Meet your group in the hallway and go in together.

- *Build awareness of early childhood and family issues.* Know the facts about your community and program.

- *Listen carefully.* Be open to questions. If you do not have information, politely explain that you will do more research and get back with some answers.

- *Ask for support for your issues.* If your legislator does not make a commitment, tactfully state that you would like to know about her or his decision and that you will call after she or he has had time to give it more thought.

- *Follow up.* Send a thank-you letter to your legislator and to the staff member who helped arrange the visit. Include a summary of your position on the issue plus any new information from your community.

- *Maintain contact.* Regularly provide information about children's and family issues.

Adapted from *Your Legislative Guide to Advocacy* by the National PTA, Edited by M.B. Oakes, 1987, Washington, DC: National PTA Office of Governmental Relations.

cate told her program staff about her visit to the capital; several teachers then volunteered to visit the legislator.

You can also write articles for your local professional newsletter or speak at a conference. An early childhood advocate in Virginia gave a conference presentation discussing her feelings about visiting a legislator and outlining some strategies she used. As a result, a group of students at the session developed a course to encourage advocacy among other early childhood students.

Several organizations now hold special legislative forums or lobbying days in conjunction with their conferences to encourage early childhood advocates to visit their legislators (see "Advocates in Action," p. 49).

In California, an annual Legislative Symposium for Children is held at the state capital. From small beginnings, this event has grown to a gathering of about 1,500 people. A full day of seminars, workshops, and visits, and lunch with legislators and aides, involves novice and experienced early childhood advocates (M. Fochler, personal correspondence, December 1987).

Influencing administrative decisions

Early childhood advocates can play a key role in shaping administrative decisions about budgets, regulations, program monitoring, and planning and reporting.

Budget priorities

Although only the legislature can appropriate funds, the budget involves both the administrative and legislative branches of government. This complex process generally begins when the chief executive submits a proposed budget to the legislature. At the federal level, this budget is submitted in January for the next fiscal year, which begins on the first day of the following October. State and local jurisdictions may follow a different timetable, but the process is often similar.

Prior to submitting its budget, an administration works for months with its agencies and budget office to project needed funds. The administration's budget reflects both existing laws and authorizations and the chief executive's priorities. The budget is usually presented to the legislature at the beginning of the session, along with a message from the president or governor.

Your budget advocacy efforts probably will begin by attempting to influence the administration's priorities. This process may actu-

Advocates in Action

New York advocates keep decision makers informed about early childhood issues

In February 1988, 3,000 child care advocates in New York went to the state capital to visit legislators as part of Day Care Education Day, organized by the New York State Child Care Coordinating Council (NYSCCCC). This annual event is the culmination of months of community activity to encourage people to let their legislators know that child care is everybody's concern.

In the fall prior to the event, representatives of the local day care councils statewide meet to determine their legislative priorities for the following session. They target specific issues and try to focus on three or four priorities. NYSCCCC staff then write up the priorities and have them printed on flyers and postcards. Thousands of these postcards are distributed to advocates across the state. The advocates pass them out to child care professionals, parents, and other community members, who mail them to their legislators at the beginning of the session. The legislative network of 100 people representing a variety of groups, including unions and church and women's groups, also helps distribute the flyers and postcards.

At the same time, meetings with various child care groups in local communities encourage people to come to the state capital for the event. On or before the day of the event, participants receive a briefing on the issues and what to tell legislators.

The day begins with a breakfast with legislators. Participants present the legislators with the child care priorities and give them packets of information and fact sheets of statistics that resource and referral agencies statewide have collected.

The day continues with further briefings in the morning and a massive gathering of all participants at the state legislative building at noon. Advocates bring signs to show their strength. In 1988, a master of ceremonies was invited to drum up spirit, and a strong advocate kicked off the event. Legislators and administrative officials also spoke at this time. In the afternoon, participants visited legislators.

This event sends a very strong message to decision makers that child care advocates intend to be heard. In 1987, despite the fact that there was no new money in the Governor's budget for child care, advocates won $14 million in new funding.

Based on a telephone interview with Louise Stoney, January 1988

49

ally precede the election. Fact sheets and statistics on children's and families' needs can inform administrators' budget decisions.

If you are dealing with an administration that is strongly opposed to your issues, it may be more effective to try to influence the legislature. Once that body receives the budget, administrative officials work to convince the legislature and relevant committees to accept the administration's proposal. These officials often testify in front of budget and appropriation committees. At this time, advocates may also be called to testify in support of or opposition to the administration's budget.

Again, it is important to know your facts on the needs and effects of certain programs. As the budget makes its way through the legislature and moves on for executive action, mobilize networks in support of or opposition to it.

Regulations

A second major function of administrative agencies is to develop rules and regulations that govern program implementation. Some of these regulations are tied to funding (such as the Head Start Program Performance Standards); others serve as minimum protection for the general public (such as state licensing standards) and may or may not affect funding.

Administrative agency staff generally draft the regulations, sometimes with advice from experts. Once regulations are drafted, they usually are sent out for public comment. At the federal level, the draft regulations are printed in the *Federal Register* as a Notice of Proposed Rulemaking. The public then has 60 days to comment before the regulation becomes part of the administrative code. Written comments from advocates on draft standards are essential to influence the final regulations.

Often, public hearings are held on draft regulations. Advocates can present testimony to support or oppose the regulations. The times and places of hearings are sometimes listed in newspapers and agency publications, but it is frequently difficult for advocates to mobilize their efforts to testify due to short notice or lack of information about the hearing.

If you are interested in testifying on pending regulations, try to maintain regular contact with administrative officials. Then you are more likely to receive information far enough in advance to adequately prepare a response. (See the section on testifying for further tips on how to prepare testimony, pp. 52–55.)

Once regulations are promulgated, you can still continue to provide input and suggest changes. By law, some regulations must be regularly reviewed and updated. In other cases, if there is a loud enough voice of concern from the public, there may be legislative or judicial action to open up the issue and revise the regulations.

Program monitoring

Administrators implement and monitor program funding and compliance with regulations. Agencies that fund programs may develop specific guidelines for distribution of funds and monitor their use. These agencies may be the same or different than the agency that regulates or licenses programs. Policy decisions may be made at the federal, state, or local level. Local agencies most often monitor implementation of guidelines.

If you are an advocate working toward changes in the monitoring process, ask yourself these questions:

- What agencies fund and monitor the programs?
- Who are the key players (agency directors and local people who review these programs)?
- What type of action do I think is needed? Changes in reporting requirements? Regulation changes? Or . . . ?
- Who is the best person to initiate action? What position will this person take?
- What recourse is available if no action is taken (other key decision makers, citizen groups, legislators, courts)?

If you intend to change the monitoring process, guidelines, or regulations, you need accurate information on how revisions will affect people and programs in your community. Then you will need to present this information clearly to the decision maker who has the most power to make the improvements.

Planning and reporting

Many administrative agencies plan new programs, study specific issues, and report their findings and recommendations to the chief executive and/or the legislature. The administration and legislature often use these reports to establish priorities.

Your influence on these reports can help ensure they include recommendations that support early childhood issues. You can contact the administrative staff who draft the reports and any advisory groups studying the issues. Be prepared to share facts and anecdotal information that support your position. Ask questions and make constructive suggestions if the group is receptive.

After reports are released, take the time to comment, especially if the report recommends priorities that you support or oppose. Direct your comments to the agency official who signed the report, and send copies to the chief executive and legislators involved.

Testifying at hearings

Hearings provide another forum for advocates to share their expertise. Different kinds of hearings are

- *Legislative* hearings at the federal, state, and local levels on specific legislation, budget items, or emerging issues.
- *Administrative* hearings, at all levels, on rules and regulations or on proposals to respond to a specific issue.
- *Judicial* hearings on pending legal issues.
- *Local hearings or public forums* held by school boards, commissions, advisory boards, or other local governing bodies or civic groups.
- *Hearings held by advocacy groups* designed to bring an issue to the public's attention.

Your testimony not only allows you to express your opinion face-to-face with the primary people involved in decision making, but often sets the stage for you to answer specific questions that may be particularly controversial. In the course of developing your testimony, you or your group may want to formally adopt a position on an issue based on research that supports that position.

You may testify as an individual, or you may speak on behalf of a group. If you represent a group, make sure your testimony stays within the positions adopted by the group.

Many hearings are held on short notice and with limited publicity. You will be able to respond in a timely manner if you already have established a communication network, are aware of position statements, and have your facts well organized. You may have to mobilize quickly.

In Minnesota, for instance, state AEYC members had worked for years to support differentiated staffing requirements for infant-toddler, preschool, and after-school child care staff in the state's licensing requirements. A draft of the regulations still did not in-

When Writing Your Testimony

- *Briefly introduce yourself.* Tell who you are and, if appropriate, what program or organization you represent. Acknowledge your appreciation to the panel for the opportunity to express your opinion or for inviting you. Indicate how many people you represent, how many people you serve, and your successes and experience in the community. Limit your introductory remarks to one or two parargraphs.

- *State your goal and major points.* Tell the group what you hope to accomplish. Be brief. Outline your major points, thereby assuring others that you are organized and that your testimony is relevant.

  For example, if the subject is exemptions to licensing regulations, indicate that you are going to provide (1) how many children and programs exemptions affect, (2) examples of health and safety risks to children caused by exemptions, (3) the extent of support against exemptions, and (4) recommendations to solve the problem.

- *Stick to the problem and geographic area.* Discuss significant issues and relate them to your state or community. If you are testifying at a legislative hearing, try to relate examples to the districts the legislators in attendance represent. Back up facts with personal stories that demonstrate how real children and families are affected by the issue.

- *Draw a broader picture.* What are other states doing? What positions have professional organizations taken? For the exemptions issue, you might point out the number of states that do not have exemptions and present NAEYC's position statement on licensing.

- *Offer specific recommendations.* Provide a concise list of what the group you are addressing can do to help solve the problem. Be realistic and positive.

- *Thank the group.* Summarize your major points and offer to answer questions.

Adapted from *Washington Workbook for Child Advocates 100th Congress 1987-1988* by the Child Welfare League of America, 1987, Washington, DC: Author. Copyright 1987 by the Child Welfare League of America. Adapted by permission.

corporate the group's recommendations. Shortly after the draft was circulated, a hearing was planned. On the day of the hearing, the AEYC public policy committee met in the morning to draft a statement, had their board approve it in the afternoon, and testified at the hearing later in the day (D. Gartrell, personal interview, January 1988). At the state and local levels, advocates may need to act this fast to participate in the policy process.

When preparing testimony, consider both the type and subject of the hearing to be held and the specific rules governing the hearing (see "When Writing Your Testimony," p. 53). If you are to testify before a local hearing, you may want to focus on local issues and concerns rather than presenting a national or state perspective. If you appear before a judicial hearing, you may be called upon to share your expertise within a format determined by an attorney. An administrative hearing on regulations may be limited to the specifics of those regulations.

Review the public notice announcing the hearing, or contact the committee or office in charge to find out

- Who can testify? Some hearings allow only invited speakers to testify; others are open to the public.
- Do you need to sign up to testify? When and where? Sometimes a list of speakers is prepared in advance. If you sign up at the hearing, arrive early to avoid being cut off if there is a limit to the number of people allowed to speak.
- How long do you have to make your points? Prepare a brief version of your testimony in case you must limit your remarks.
- Where do you submit your written testimony? Oral testimony should be written, too. Make enough copies for everyone attending. An official may preside, or a clerk may receive written testimony after it is presented. You may want to prepare a news release for any journalists present.
- Who will represent your group? Select someone who is an effective speaker and who knows the facts. Sometimes several group members will testify, each on a different aspect of the position.

Your speaking style often strongly influences the impact of your message. Talk to the committee in a conversational way rather than reading to or speaking at them. Limit yourself to 5 or 10 minutes. Committee members may not be experts—so avoid educational jargon.

One good way to catch the attention of committee members is to "speak media" ("How To Lobby," 1985). Try coming up with a simple sentence or phrase that captures the essence of your issue and gives committee members an image to remember. For example:

> Several years ago, the California legislature was considering a bill to establish child care programs in each of the state's migrant farm worker housing camps. The child advocate spoke media: She came up with the image of babies in crates at the end of each furrow. She began her testimony at each hearing with the line: "Gentlemen, we need this bill because right now, as we sit in air-conditioned comfort, there are babies in crates at the end of each furrow. . . ." By the time the bill reached the floor of the legislature for final consideration, legislators had made the phrase their own. ("How To Lobby," 1985, p. 10)

Do not be intimidated by the size of the room or the power of the people up on the podium. You are the expert. Be confident, believe in your cause, and step forward to testify.

Becoming involved in political campaigns

> If we are the only group that is too busy for politics, then our children will be the only group that is ignored in the political process. If we are too afraid or proud or uninformed to participate in politics, then legislators will interpret our silence as consent, no matter what they do to children. (Children's Defense Fund, 1983, p. 1)

Too many politicians continue to ignore critical issues that affect young children and their families. If you—and all early childhood professionals—became more actively involved in the election process, we could make important political connections and family and children's issues would command greater priority (see "Advocates in Action," p. 56).

How can you get involved? First, you can make sure you vote in elections. Next, you can give financial or volunteer support to candidates who have worked in favor of children and families. You can also become involved with local political parties and raise early childhood issues with candidates. Nonprofit organizations have limitations on their involvement in political campaigns. As an individual constituent, however, you have the right to become involved in elections and to support the candidates of your choice.

Advocates in Action

Massachusetts advocates stand up for their profession

In the early 1980s, advocates in Massachusetts began raising the issue of increasing child care salaries with legislators. Although initial attempts to pass a child care minimum wage bill were not successful, this effort did allow advocates the opportunity to voice their concern over inadequate salaries with legislative committees that had not addressed the issue in the past.

During the following gubernatorial election, advocates decided to become actively involved in supporting a candidate for governor who was supportive of child care issues. Advocates set up an endorsement meeting, questioned candidates on child care issues, obtained commitments from a candidate, contributed to the campaign, and were successful in helping to elect a governor who was sympathetic to child care issues.

Once elected, the governor established the Day Care Partnership Project, which included a diverse group of leaders from human services, business, the legislature, labor, philanthropy, and child care, who were brought together to develop a comprehensive child care policy for the state. Because of the efforts of child care workers across the state, wage proposals, briefly mentioned in the plan's preliminary recommendations, were made an integral part of the governor's recommendations.

As a result of these and other efforts, advocates in Massachusetts have been able to secure millions of dollars in state funds to upgrade the salaries of child care and Head Start workers, as well as additional funds to make child care more affordable. Studies indicate that the state supplemental grants for salary increases made a difference in the ability to recruit and retain qualified staff. The efforts of Massachusetts advocates, standing up for increased compensation for child care staff, has become a landmark in the movement to speak out for better working conditions and increased salaries and benefits for early childhood employees across the country.

Based on a telephone interview with Nancy DeProsse, January 1988

Never assume that other advocates share the same knowledge and skills. If your newsletter asks people to volunteer to testify, for example, list the phone number and name of the person to call, or the time at which people are expected to sign up to appear on the agenda. Organizers must consider the prerequisite knowledge advocates need to be successful.

Do not limit communications only to members. Send your newsletter to public officials, administrators, and others who share your interest or who can learn from your materials. Offer to write columns for other newsletters. This helps develop a broader base of people concerned about children's and family issues.

Giving presentations at meetings and professional conferences enables you to keep noninvolved community members, decision makers, and group members informed about issues. Presentations with this focus are usually held during professional conferences or at meetings specifically organized to focus on an issue.

Direct your material to the issue (see the section on speaking to local groups later in this chapter for additional tips). Be sure to explain how the information was gathered, how it is being used, how advocates can use the information, and how to contact you after the meeting. A one-page handout should summarize the information for future reference.

Action alerts and telephone trees enable you to quickly inform members about needed action, usually on legislation. Their purpose is to generate phone calls, cards, and letters supporting a bill at critical stages of the legislative process. Both depend upon the people contacted to act on the information. When developing a list of who should receive either style of communication, therefore, be sure to choose people who are comfortable writing to or talking with their legislators.

Action alerts are one-page flyers—brief and to the point. They provide information, outline action for readers to take, and usually include a deadline for acting. Alerts are only effective if a member of the group stays informed about a bill's status and the most effective kind of response needed for its passage. A disadvantage of alerts is the absence of a feedback mechanism; there is no sure way of knowing how many advocates responded to the call for action. In addition, funds are needed for typing, duplicating, and mailing the alert. An advantage is the ability to contact quickly a large number of advocates about the need for immediate action.

There are many examples of action emerging across the country as early childhood professionals and parents of young children become more politically minded. Advocates in Oregon developed a pre-election candidate survey that included 10 early childhood issues. They discussed these issues with candidates running for state office. In Virginia, advocates developed a list of questions to ask candidates about state child care issues. Copies of the questions were distributed at the state AEYC conference so individual members could use the questions when candidates held meetings in their district.

Similar activities can take place with candidates running for national office. Phillips and Lande (1988) contacted all the presidential candidates in 1988. They suggest that you follow suit in any election. Write a short letter to the candidates and ask them for their positions on child and family issues. Tell the candidate you vote, and that you will vote for the individual with the best and clearest position on the issues.

We can also become candidates ourselves—seeking political or appointed positions with governments, councils, commissions, and advisory boards. In state and local areas, an increasing number of early childhood professionals are seeing this as an important option for effecting change. We should lend our support to our colleagues who can make this important commitment.

Talking with employers

In the past decade, employers have begun to recognize how child care and other family issues affect parents at work. It is important for early childhood advocates to reach out to businesses to encourage private sector support of programs and services. Many employers also have political influence in the community and therefore can lend critical support to our efforts.

When child care is unreliable, parents have trouble getting to work on time. They may have to leave early or even miss days. Even at work, they can be worried or preoccupied about their children's care. But the effects of child care problems do not stop there. Problems, especially dealing with child care arrangements that break down frequently, can have an impact on employed parents' mental and physical health, even on their perceived competence as parents and their satisfaction with life. (Galinsky, 1987)

Use your expertise about these issues to build awareness about the relationship between work and family life. Before approaching employers, find out which employers in your community already offer employees some type of family-support benefits (on-site care, vouchers, flexible work hours, job sharing). Identify business leaders and early childhood experts in your community who are already involved in efforts to encourage policies that support families.

Next, decide whether you want to talk with a specific employer or a group of employers (such as business groups, organizations that employ the parents in your program, nearby establishments, employers with large numbers of workers, producers or distributors of products for families and children).

Decide what the purpose of your contact is. Are you seeking

- to obtain financial support to improve a particular aspect of your program?
- to inform employers about the range of options regarding family services? If you are a provider, how can your program help?
- to showcase model programs in the community already supported by other businesses?
- to advise managers about the conflicts today's families face and how supervisors can deal more effectively with these problems?
- to offer parent education or parent support groups for the company's employees?
- to enlist corporate support for a particular public policy that affects children and families (parental leave or child care support)?

If you are approaching a group of employers, you may want to write letters to their corporate executives, personnel departments, or public relations offices to see whether they are interested in your ideas. When you write, remember to introduce yourself, establish your expertise, and clearly state the reason for the contact. As with any advocacy initiative, your efforts may be more productive if someone inside the organization can lead you to the best person to contact. (For more information about approaching employers, see NAEYC's *Employer-Assisted Child Care Resource Guide* and *Information Kit on Employer-Assisted Child Care*.)

Contacting the media

Television, radio, magazines, newspapers, and community newsletters—all are important tools to shape public opinion on child and family issues. For too long, these influential tools have intimidated many of us, and too often we remain uninformed about how to use the media to our advantage (Friedman, Ginsburg, & Whitebook, 1984).

Tune in to what local reporters are covering. What is making the news? Who are the people who shape the topics and angles presented? Read your local newspapers, magazines, and newsletters and listen to radio and television news and talk shows to find out what seems to be of current interest in your community.

As you tune in to the news, develop a list of key media contacts: names, addresses, and telephone numbers for newspaper reporters and editors (especially those who write on family issues); call letters, frequencies, addresses, and telephone numbers of all local radio and television stations. Call and ask for the names of the producers of public affairs, interview, and talk shows. Note the bylines in newspapers and the credits at the end of TV programs.

Once you are familiar with local reporting and resources, you can begin to respond to the news. Take advantage of letters to the editor, editorials, and guest columns. If you write a letter immediately after a story has appeared, you may be able to influence an editorial on the topic.

Letters to the editor are one of the most frequently read sections of a newspaper or magazine. NAEYC's *Making News: An Affiliate Guide to Working With the News Media* (1987) provides these **tips for writing letters to the editor:**

- Mail your letter the day the story appears.
- Pick one or two important points and make them briefly. Succinct letters are more likely to be printed.
- Published letters are rarely more than three paragaphs long, so expect portions to be cut.
- Sign your name, and identify yourself if it is relevant to the issue. Cite your professional organization only if it has taken a similar position.

Advocates in Action

Missouri advocate seizes an opportunity to act

During the fall of 1986, child care made front page headlines in a major Kansas City newspaper. Because child care was often portrayed negatively, a local advocate called the reporter to try to provide a more balanced picture. The phone call led to a meeting.

The reporter found the information presented by the advocate so interesting she suggested the advocate organize a conference on the issue. The advocate in turn asked if the newspaper would fund such an activity. The newspaper had already spent its funds for sponsoring such events, but the idea for a conference had been launched; the date was set, and the reporter agreed to cover the event.

As the advocate discussed the idea with others, it was decided that the conference would focus on a variety of perspectives on child care, including parents', professionals', and employers'. Recognizing the need for services and financial support, the advocate contacted community groups and businesses that represented these various perspectives. The local parents' magazine agreed to provide refreshments and funds for mailing; the University of Missouri/Kansas City provided the meeting hall. Financial support came from local children's ser-vices organizations, local businesses, and affiliates of national children's and women's organizations. The advocate frequently called upon others for assistance and always found them willing to contribute to the effort.

The half-day invitational conference took place in December 1987. Legislators, parents, community decision makers, and child care professionals were invited. They heard a nationally known speaker on family issues and two panels representing various perspectives on child care and then met in small groups to discuss the issues. The conference was audiotaped and transcribed. Participants received a copy of the transcript.

Local papers and television stations covered the event, providing a more complete picture of child care. Participants grew in their understanding of the complexities of the issues. Advocates and organizations formed new linkages. The conference mailing list was later used to inform people about the Act for Better Child Care. New groups have become involved with local child care initiatives as a result of the conference.

Based on a telephone interview with Stacie Goffin, February 1988

Another approach is to call the editor about submitting an editorial or a guest column in response to a story. These pieces are often written by local experts—so establish your credibility and availability.

You can also take the opportunity to talk with reporters either in response to a story or to initiate an item (see "Advocates in Action," p. 60). The goal is to keep your issues in front of the public to build awareness (see "When You Are Interviewed or Ask To Talk With Reporters," p. 62). In fact, the news may provide you with a local key to use to get your message across. In one community, a fire broke out in a licensed family day care home that enrolled more than 10 children. Local advocates, who for years had been trying to limit the number of children in group care, used the opportunity to talk with reporters about their issue. Several stories followed that examined state and local licensing requirements and the need for legislative change.

Other publications to help your work with the media, advocates, and others are in Appendix G.

References

Allen, K.E. (1983). Children, the Congress, and you. *Young Children, 38*(2), 71–75.

Beck, R. (1979). *It's time to stand up for your children: A parent's guide to child advocacy.* Washington, DC: Children's Defense Fund.

Children's Defense Fund. (1983). *Lobbying and political activity for nonprofits.* Washington, DC: Author.

Friedman, J., Ginsburg, G., & Whitebook, M. (1984). *Managing the media maze.* Berkeley, CA: Child Care Employee Project.

Galinsky, E. (1987, January). *The impact of child care problems on parents on the job and at home.* Presentation at the Wingspread Conference, Child Care Action Committee, Racine, WI.

Goffin, S.G., with Caccomo, J. (1986). *In partnership with parents.* Jefferson City, MO: State Department of Education, Division of Special Education.

Hostetler, L. (1983, March/April). How-to guide for advocates. *Child Care Information Exchange,* pp. 25–29.

How To Lobby for Child Care. (1985, May). *Child Care Information Exchange,* pp. 9–10.

National Association for the Education of Young Children. (1987). *Making news: An Affiliate guide to working with the news media.* Washington, DC: Author. (Out of print).

Phillips, D.A., & Lande, J. (1988, January). The politics of child care. *Child Care Information Exchange,* pp. 9–12.

Pizzo, P. (1983). *Parent to parent.* Boston: Beacon.

Tyler-Wilkins, A., & Blank, H. (1987). Building a child care coalition and giving it power. In *Child Care America: Project guidelines and resources for community organization and outreach activity* (pp. 67–77). (A National Project of the Public Television Outreach Alliance).

Wilkins, A., & Blank, H. (1986). Child care: Strategies to move the issue forward. *Young Children, 42*(1), 68–72.

When You Are Interviewed or Ask To Talk With Reporters

- Know exactly what information you want reported before you seek the interview. Limit yourself to two or three main points.

- Refer to these points throughout the discussion—not just once. Relate them to important facts and personal-interest stories.

- If the reporter does not ask about a significant area, volunteer the information. "There's one area we haven't touched on that is very important and that is. . . ."

- Stick to your area of expertise. If you do not know an answer, say so. If you can find out, tell the reporter you will call with the information, and then follow through.

- Above all, avoid jargon or ambiguous thoughts. If only a technical word seems to fit, then explain its meaning. If the ideas are complex, rephrase the idea in another way: "Let me make sure I made myself clear. . . ."

- Adjust your rate of speaking to the reporter's ability to record what you are saying.

- If you are doing a TV interview, write your response out first in no more than three simple sentences. Generally speaking, your answer has the best chance of being used if it is between 20 and 30 seconds long.

- Suggest related stories, but if no interest is expressed, don't persist.

- After the interview, if you realize you made a factual mistake, call the reporter and correct your error. The reporter will have more, not less, regard for your credibility.

Adapted from NAEYC's *Making News: An Affiliate Guide to Working With the News Media,* 1987. (Out of print).

Chapter 4

Joining With Others To Reach Your Goals

A dvocates join with others because together they can accomplish changes that cannot be achieved by individuals acting alone. In addition, a shared message has much more weight and impact. Sheer numbers can sometimes lead to changes that even the most persistent individual could not bring about.

Working with others allows advocates to pool their expertise. This way, no one person has to do it all and each person gets to do what she or he does best and enjoys most. The expanded range of skills and knowledge improves the chances that the group will reach its goals. Working with others also links colleagues who can share moral support, encouragement, and feedback.

Collaborating with other groups

You might join with other early childhood advocates as an individual or as a representative of another membership group such as a professional association or employee organization. You can participate in networks, coalitions, advisory boards, or commissions or task forces.

These groups form at each level of advocacy—local, state, and national—but differ in their purposes and what they can accomplish most successfully. When you choose to join with others, you must decide what you want to achieve and which group most closely shares your goals.

Membership organizations

A number of membership organizations provide professional development opportunities for educators of young children. Some groups focus on early childhood issues (NAEYC and its affiliates, child care employee groups); others have a broader concern with members from diverse professional backgrounds (American Association of University Women, National Urban League). Some of these groups are listed in Appendix F. By overlapping your memberships, you can build linkages with other organizations and thus gain wider support from a greater number of people. Being able to tell policymakers and other decision makers that your efforts represent 200 members, for example, strengthens your impact. State employees in Pennsylvania, for instance, successfully lobbied for early childhood services through their employee organization, which included early childhood professionals (Halpern, 1981).

Many membership organizations, including AEYC groups, rely on volunteers to achieve their purposes. Members' continued commitment depends upon their receiving personal as well as professional satisfaction from their efforts. Because members have different interests and are at different levels of involvement in their professional growth (Smith, 1987), groups will vary in their priorities and the activities they prefer to support. You may even need to convince your colleagues that policy decisions have an important effect on children's growth and that one of their professional responsibilities should include involvement in advocacy.

One way a group can actualize its commitment to advocacy is by designating an Advocacy or Public Policy Committee (although advocacy efforts need not be limited to public policy advocacy). This committee should provide a focus as well as an action plan for the group's efforts.

The committee's success depends in large part upon selecting a chairperson whose interests, skills, and abilities are consistent with the challenges associated with advocacy. An advocacy chairperson must be able to act as a mentor for emerging advocates, support active advocates, and conceptualize the organization's activities within an advocacy framework. A chairperson can facilitate these goals by bringing information to the membership, helping the group focus on specific issues, recommending advocacy strategies, and organizing others to act.

Focus is crucial—it is easy to be distracted by all the needs of children and those who care for them. The advocacy committee should select an issue that is consistent with the organization's purpose, interests, and planning process and should develop specific strategies to move the issue forward. Flip-flopping from one issue to another, or taking on too many at once, dilutes a group's efforts and undermines its effectiveness.

An advocacy committee can help governing boards and the general membership to structure their advocacy focus in at least three ways:

1. platform statements

2. resolutions

3. position statements

Platform statements are an advocacy tool for helping a group focus and prioritize its concerns. They are adopted by the governing board and written as specifically as possible to describe the group's preferred solution to a problem. For example, "_____ organization supports improved licensing standards that address group size, teacher/child ratios, caregiver training, and program criteria." In contrast, a sweeping statement supporting developmentally appropriate programs is too general and open to misinterpretation. Platforms can help a group (or its lobbyist) respond to proposed public policies.

Resolutions are formal expressions of an organization's commitment and concern and thus should be consistent with the group's platform. Resolutions are adopted by the governing board and/or full membership as an expression of a decision to act in a particular way.

Resolutions most often appear in the format

"Whereas, . . .

    Therefore, . . ."

and are rarely longer than one page. The "whereas" sections contain statements of facts and/or beliefs; the "therefore" portion sets forth the action or position based on those facts and beliefs. For example, "Whereas _____ organization believes in maximizing the support systems available to families with infants, therefore _____ organization supports restoring $100,000 in state funds for maternal and infant care programs." The impact of resolutions is maximized by disseminating them to policymakers and others involved with the issue.

Position statements are summaries of evidence with conclusions and recommendations (A.D.A. Reports, 1980; Masters, 1984). Position statements can be organized and written in a variety of styles.

They usually include a rationale, definitions of frequently used terms, a review of relevant literature, recommendations for change, and references. Position statements provide a framework for further action on an issue, such as letters to legislators or newspaper editors, responses to proposed regulations, or testimony preparation.

Groups usually adopt a position statement when they (1) confront an issue of concern to their membership and (2) are willing to take a stand, but (3) lack a clear, well-organized document that represents their stance and that can be used to educate others. A committee usually prepares the statement by reviewing the literature and talking with experts.

When a position statement is approved, it assumes the weight of the group accepting it. Its political clout extends beyond the viewpoint of a single individual or a small group. Position statements can be strengthened when jointly developed by several groups or endorsed by other groups upon completion. Position statements are especially effective tools for increasing public understanding of an issue and informing public- and private-sector decision making.

Developing platforms, resolutions, and position statements reflects an organization's growing sophistication in advocacy. However, an advocacy committee may initially need to focus its efforts on nurturing its own members' increased involvement in advocacy activity and educating them about issues and specific advocacy skills. As developmentally oriented educators already know, the starting point for growth is with the individual.

Networks

Most networks are informal groups that meet regularly to share information. Members are usually representatives from professional organizations, labor groups, agencies, and institutions that work with or on behalf of young children—rather than unaffiliated individuals.

Groups can easily become isolated. This isolation sometimes fosters competition and distrust among groups that work with or on behalf of a similar population of children or who compete for the same resources. Participation in a network helps reduce an organization's sense of isolation, increase members' awareness of others' activities, and break down misconceptions and communication barriers that may exist. As a result, networks are an advocacy technique that fosters relationships (Morgan, 1983) that may, in turn, be involved later in more focused advocacy activity.

Because of their informality, networks usually require few formal policies and have a flexible organizational structure. One or two leaders often set the meeting dates, organize their location, arrange speakers, keep members informed, and facilitate the meeting's flow.

Networks create a nonthreatening environment in which participants can exchange information and become more aware of each other's viewpoints (Briggs, 1985). A network's success is based primarily upon the equality of its members, the absence of additional responsibilities, and the opportunity for people to get to know each other and be better informed about relevant issues and events. Because networks focus on establishing relationships and new allies, their impact usually increases with time (see "Advocates in Action," p. 70).

Coalitions

Coalitions or alliances are organized gatherings of representatives from groups that have decided to plan and coordinate their efforts to achieve a specific purpose. Once that purpose is achieved, many coalitions are dismantled, although members often stay in touch about other advocacy efforts. Some coalitions even evolve into permanent advocacy groups. Coalitions, therefore, may differ from networks in their structure, purpose, and life span.

Coalitions are usually formed to develop or respond to legislation. They serve as focal points, clearinghouses, and coordinators to make sure that participating groups and individuals are doing all they can to achieve a desired result (League of Women Voters of the United States, 1976).

Coalitions are outcome oriented. They are only as strong as their member organizations' skills, contacts, and commitment. Intense efforts are required to create and maintain a shared focus. Therefore, strong leadership, sufficient resources, and a constant focus on the desired outcome are necessary for a coalition's success (Bing & Richart, 1987).

Successful legislative campaigns depend upon the active support of a large and diverse constituency that can send a message of broad-based support to decision makers. Coalitions should include as many organizations as possible that share an interest in a par-

Advocates in Action

Montana advocates build an information network

In 1985, Montana State University, in conjunction with the Montana Association for the Education of Young Children, received a grant from the Northwest Area Foundation of St. Paul, Minnesota, to fund an Early Childhood Project to:

- identify existing programs statewide and set up a network to disseminate and coordinate information regarding early childhood issues and concerns across the state;
- explore systems for registering preschools and assist in developing recommended standards for preschool programs;
- design innovative techniques for informing parents and providers about the needs of preschoolers and early childhood services; and
- develop a videotape resource library for use with media awareness and training.

Believing it important to build grassroots support as the core to developing a statewide structure, the Early Childhood Project focused its first-year activities on developing local "child care teams." The project provided minimal funding for a local early childhood "field consultant" in

each of 13 communities to create an interagency team in the area by identifying key people in the community involved in early childhood programs. This resulted in the development of a Resource Directory of early childhood programs throughout the state.

During the second and third years, the Early Childhood Project received additional funds and funneled this money to the teams to provide early childhood training. Each community decided the content of the training based on its needs. The project also assisted the teams in developing grant-writing skills. These efforts helped to establish five new resource and referral centers in the state.

Along with building local capacity, the Early Childhood Project has provided advocates a wealth of information and resources on a wide variety of issues facing the state, has published a newsletter, has established liaisons with state and local agencies and other groups, and has supported the development of the Montana Alliance for Better Child Care.

Based on a telephone interview with Billie Warford, February 1988

ticular legislative issue, although the reasons for their interest may vary. A coalition's strength comes from its ability to activate a large number of advocates and to propose concrete initiatives in ways unorganized constituencies cannot (Hayes, 1982).

To create and maintain a shared focus, coalition members must be able to put aside their differences and focus on the desired outcome, not always an easy task. Participants need to be skilled in negotiation and compromise. People are likely to disagree on priorities, strategies, and tactics. The effort required to resolve these differences is worthwhile, however, because of the greater political impact of organized constituencies.

Coalition organizers often need to convince potential participants of the advantage of their involvement and reassure them that the coalition will not take over any of their present functions (Fried, 1983). Each group should be approached with arguments based on its own interests. In Indiana, for example, advocates for school-age child care legislation won support of local fire officials and county prosecutors by arguing that unsupervised children were more likely to hurt themselves and others than children in supervised programs (Wilkins & Blank, 1986).

Considerable leadership effort is needed to maintain members' involvement, sustain their motivation, and unite their efforts. Groups must be clear about what contributions they are expected to make and the issues they are supporting. No group should be pushed to go beyond its resources or interests. Regular communication and opportunities for members to influence group decisions are crucial. Members need to receive sincere, meaningful recognition.

Coalitions are an especially effective advocacy tool. They can become extremely sophisticated, but they require considerable time and leadership expertise (see Advocates in Action, p. 72).

Advisory boards

Many programs, such as Head Start, Health Service Agencies, and Title I of the Elementary and Secondary Education Act, require citizens' advisory boards to participate in making policy and program decisions. By becoming members of such a board, individual advocates or representatives from professional groups can share their early childhood perspective to help inform the group's decision making. Participation on advisory boards provides a direct way to influence decisions that affect children's well-being. At the same time, you assist other professionals and parents in learning more about early childhood education.

Advocates in Action

A coalition grows in Vermont

The Vermont Children's Forum (VCF) is a coalition of child advocates, educators, service providers, parents, and other concerned citizens acting together to promote services and programs for children and youth in Vermont. The Children's Forum, established in 1983, was an outgrowth of volunteer efforts begun by representatives from a wide variety of groups in the state concerned with child and family issues. Preliminary efforts included organizing a statewide conference and developing a fact book, *The Kids in Our Backyard: Some Facts You Should Know About Vermont's Children*. These efforts were launched with volunteer labor from the advocacy community along with a small grant from the state. After a year of meetings to discuss establishing an organization, the coalition decided to incorporate.

Initial funding included proceeds from the sale of the fact book and membership from individuals ($15) and organizations ($25). In 1987, VCF received its first foundation support, a grant from a local business (Ben and Jerry's Homemade Ice Cream, Inc., an ice cream manufacturer). This grant allowed VCF to launch the Vermont Children's Campaign to increase public awareness of children's and families' issues and to develop support for children's services. The campaign included a published legislative agenda, used by advocates in working for specific actions. Additional funding was secured for this project the following year along with a grant from the Vermont Children's Trust to look at primary prevention projects. The Children's Forum relies on the services of a part-time lobbyist and the strong participation of its members to effect change for children and families.

Based on a personal interview with Lee Lauber, January, 1988

Commissions and task forces

Special commissions and task forces may be appointed by government officials, professional groups, or volunteer organizations. Most task forces include staff, interested citizens, and knowledgeable professionals in their membership. Task forces usually document problems and suggest recommendations for action. These groups can generate consensus on issues and, by soliciting input from experts, introduce new possibilities (Bing & Richart, 1987).

As a member of this type of group, you have the opportunity, either as an individual or as a representative of a professional organization, to influence the direction of policymaking from within, rather than outside, the system (Kilmer, 1980). This can be an especially effective way to influence the development or revision of administrative rules and regulations.

Unfortunately, sometimes officials appoint task forces with the intent to delay real decision making while presenting an image of interest and concern. Other times, to please everyone, a group's recommendations are so watered down they are meaningless. Even if you are concerned about the nature of the group, it may still be worth getting involved if your skills and knowledge can help move the issues forward and maintain the group's direction.

Working effectively with others

Strong groups don't just happen. They emerge and grow through the efforts of many individuals. Regardless of the type of group, participants need to be in agreement about how the group will operate and what its purpose is. Tasks need to be clearly defined and assigned. There must be sufficient resources for the group to achieve its goals; otherwise, the group's goal setting may be unrealistic. Members also need strong skills in working with each other.

Choosing your most suited role

Once you decide to join a group, you can select whether you want to be a contributor, advisor, or leader. All three roles are important in any group, and, in fact, you may play each role at different times. Advocates can only be responsible for a few projects at one time, so you will need to be capable of supporting and following others' efforts, too (Smith, 1987).

Contributors are active members. They participate in decision making and help carry out the group's activities. They tend to prefer to cooperate with the leadership of others, however, rather than assume leadership responsibility.

Advisors educate others about an issue. This is an especially important role when you are involved in a group with members unfamiliar with early childhood issues. In describing her role as an advisor to a local task force, Kilmer (1980) emphasized the importance of both her early childhood expertise and her sensitivity to the political aspects of the process.

Leaders coordinate and provide the vision, focus, encouragement, support, and stamina to maintain a group's momentum. Effective leaders are critical to a group's success.

Developing awareness of group dynamics

Working with other people is not always easy. For example, groups can get mired down by an individual's personal agenda or someone's inability to cooperate (see "Games Advocates Play," p. 75). Awareness of the skills it takes to keep a group running smoothly can facilitate the group process. Effective advocacy groups know how to transform their interests into a shared vision and coordinated activity.

Promoting interpersonal skills. Advocacy efforts require understanding what will encourage others to become involved on behalf of children and creating the circumstances so that advocates can effectively express their concerns. In a group situation, this requires understanding group dynamics and the democratic process (Kilmer, 1980; Morgan, 1983; Meadors, 1984).

These understandings enable advocates to work together cooperatively. Give-and-take is an integral part of democratic group interaction, so be prepared to compromise. Each person and group has different priorities and strategies, which can cause internal conflicts. Still, it is always important to respect the ideas of others. Trying to figure out the reasons behind differences can help make them more understandable (League of Women Voters of the United States, 1976; Zigler & Finn, 1981).

It takes time to build trusting relationships among group members, so effective leaders allow ample opportunities—formal and informal—for this process to take place. They make sure everyone has time to express her or his views and chances to influence the direction of a decision. Disagreements are inevitable in a group. When they occur, be sure to fight the issues—not the people.

Keeping each other informed. Successful groups foster satisfying, trusting relationships and set achievable goals. Achieving these goals requires members to share their knowledge and keep each other informed as issues develop. Otherwise, members will not have the information needed to act and the group's advocacy effort will be undermined. Members should always be aware of what is happening, how things are progressing, and how they can help.

Games Advocates Play

The misery game. Advocates complain instead of directing their energies to finding realistic solutions to a problem.

The structure game. Too much time is spent debating differences or how the group should be organized, instead of how to make an objective achievable.

The protect-my-turf game. Advocates focus on their personal or organizational issues, needs, and prestige at the expense of others.

The conference-and-meeting game. Too many meetings and conferences become a substitute for action.

The all-talk-and-no-action game. Advocates spend too much time talking about, rather than solving, problems.

The looking-over-our-shoulders-at-what-everybody-else-is-doing game. Advocates can learn from others, but they need to spend most of their time doing, not watching.

The wait-for-everybody-to-come-along game. Not everyone will—or can—work with others to achieve a goal. Act with the resources you have, and continue to invite others to join you.

Adapted from *Building a House on the Hill for Our Children* by the Children's Public Policy Network, 1980, Washington, DC: Children's Defense Fund. Copyright 1980 by the Children's Defense Fund. Adapted by permission.

Constant telephone contact is essential among the leadership of a group advocacy effort. In addition, newsletters, presentations, and action alerts or telephone trees can help members stay informed. Each form of communication serves a different purpose and requires different kinds of resources. Communication facilitates relationships, expands the core of knowledgeable advocates, and initiates advocacy action. In general, therefore, the more frequent and broad-based the communication, the more likely the group is to feel a common sense of purpose.

Newsletters or policy columns should be attractive and marked with clear headlines to stimulate interest. Information should be descriptive without being too long, the style clear and readable. Readers should always be informed about what *they* can do: "Write or call your senators and urge them to. . . ."

Telephone trees are more complicated to organize but can activate action even more quickly than alerts. Quick response is necessary when a policymaker's support or vote is needed within 48 hours. Telephone trees work like a chain letter. A chairperson starts the process by calling the key contacts with a brief action update and a message to be phoned in to targeted legislators. These advocates, in turn, contact their legislators and then call an additional three to five members to spread the word. Ideally, no one person has to spend more than 20 or 30 minutes on the phone, yet legislators receive dozens of calls as a result.

Telephone volunteers should be organized by state and/or congressional districts. This way, when specific legislators need to be contacted, the telephone tree can alert their constituents (see Figure 4.1). Representatives are most responsive to the concerns of constituents who vote them into office.

One of the hardest parts in setting up a tree can be getting group members to locate their district number and the names of their state and federal representatives. Another challenge is to establish checkpoints to make sure the chain is not broken. In a large tree, people farther out on the branches could call the chairperson or district contact to report receiving their call. At a minimum, the last person on each branch should notify the chair or district contact that the chain was completed.

Just as with alerts, the chairperson and district contacts need to be well informed about the proposed legislation and its progress. Callers need to be able to answer the questions of others in the chain and to explain the needed action. A contingency plan should be developed so callers know how to "jump over" an unavailable link. Weak links in the chain should be replaced or put at the end of the chain. Telephone trees require careful coordination to keep all the parts functioning.

Reaching out to the community

Groups can be especially effective in building community awareness and support for children's issues by planning special events and organizing a speakers' bureau. The recent increased attention to early childhood concerns makes these kinds of efforts especially viable strategies. Reaching out to other groups is an effective way to enlarge constituency concern and support for early childhood issues.

Figure 4.1
Telephone Tree Outline

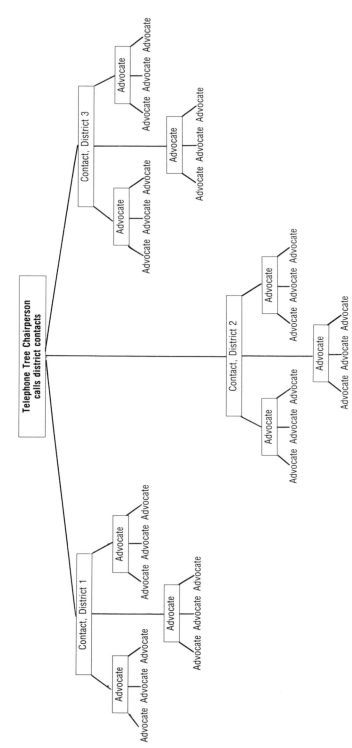

Planning special events

A variety of events can increase public awareness of early childhood issues.

Conferences, workshops, and seminars build awareness of specific issues and help participants plan strategies for action.

Celebrations, festivals, or fairs bring children, parents, and educators together for a good time. They can provide attention for an issue such as appropriate early education practices.

Shopping mall activities/exhibits can increase your group's visibility as well as public sensitivity to early childhood issues.

Open houses and tours of early childhood programs enable parents and the general public to become better informed about good early childhood programs.

Although public events can be planned throughout the year, they are especially appropriate for the Week of the Young Child. This week, usually celebrated in April, is sponsored by NAEYC. Its purpose is to help people focus attention on the needs of young children and their families.

All of these events take a great deal of planning, effort, and cooperation. As part of the planning process, it is important to identify your goals, select the kind of event most likely to achieve those goals, and obtain the necessary resources (sites, volunteers, financial support). Evaluate the event afterward so that when you plan the next one, you learn from your experiences.

Speaking to local groups

Every community has civic, church, labor, political, and special interest groups—Junior League, Rotary Club, Chamber of Commerce, Knights of Columbus, unions, and many more. With the growing attention to children's issues, many of these groups are interested in hearing local experts present information on the topic.

A speakers' bureau can be a resource for informing community groups about important early childhood issues. Speakers' bureaus arrange for speakers on a variety of topics and help connect them with interested groups. If possible, speakers should represent a wide range of child- and family-related professions: psychologists, health workers, and children's librarians, for example. This increases constituency support for your issues. The formation of your service can be announced by developing a short press release. Publicize your speakers' bureau by sending letters to area church and civic groups, clubs, and associations.

Before planning a speakers' bureau, however, first determine community interest in such a project. The Chamber of Commerce can identify professional and civic organizations that could be surveyed for their interest.

Forming a speakers' bureau may be too ambitious for your group. If you are still interested in making some direct contacts, you could arrange individual speaking engagements.

Individual and bureau presentations should match the interests of audience organizations. If you are interested in building coalitions, for example, focus on religious, labor, and women's groups; if you are interested in expanding employer support for child care, address business groups. Contact the president or program chairperson. Introduce yourself, establish your expertise, state your goals, and provide a brief summary of your proposed presentation. If the group is interested, agree upon a date and inquire about length of time, format, and facilities.

To enhance your presentation, consider displaying pictures of children and families or preparing eye-catching charts to illustrate your points. Handouts should be kept to a minimum so the audience doesn't have to fumble with papers. Make sure your message is clear, especially if you are asking the group to take some action on an issue.

For clarity, avoid professional jargon and try to keep your remarks brief. It's helpful to have a shorter version of your presentation ready to deliver if your time is cut short. At the end, ask for questions and answers. These often catch the attention of the audience better than prepared speeches. Remember to thank the group for the opportunity to speak, both at the end of the talk and in a follow-up letter.

* * * * *

Early childhood advocates working together can accomplish much for children and families. Our efforts to reach out to others will need to be continuous so we can tackle the many issues still to be resolved.

References

A.D.A. Reports. (1980, August). A position paper on position papers. *Journal of the American Dietetic Association, 77,* 179–181.

Bing, S. R., & Richart, D. W. (1987). *Fairness is a kid's game: A background paper for child advocates.* Indianapolis: The Lilly Endowment, Inc. Available from Kentucky Youth Advocates, Inc., 2024 Woodford Pl., Louisville, KY 40205.

Briggs, P. (1985). The early childhood network—We work together for young children. *Young Children, 40*(5), 54–55.

Fried, M. (1983). Coalition building for children. *Young Children, 38*(4), 77–80.

Halpern, R. (1981, August). *Assuring quality early childhood service: The challenge ahead.* A report on the conference "State Commitments to Young Children," Clinton, MI. Available from Center for the Study of Public Policies for Young Children, High/Scope Educational Research Foundation, 600 N. River St., Ypsilanti, MI 48197.

Hayes, C. D. (Ed.). (1982). *Making policies for children: A study of the federal process.* Washington, DC: National Academic Press.

Kilmer, S. (1980). Early childhood specialists as policymakers. *Education and Urban Society, 12,* 241–251.

League of Women Voters of the United States. (1976). *Making an issue of it: The campaign handbook.* Washington, DC: Author.

Masters, J. C. (1984). Models for training and research in child development and social policy. In G. J. Whitehurst (Ed.), *Annals of child development* (Vol. 1, pp. 263–301). Greenwich, CT: JAI Press.

Meadors, H. (1984). Interagency cooperation: The sum is greater than its parts. *Dimensions, 12*(3), 29–30.

Morgan, G. G. (1983). Practical techniques for change. *Journal of Children in Contemporary Society, 15*(4), 91–103.

Smith, M. M. (1987). NAEYC at 60: Visions for the year 2000. *Young Children, 42*(3), 33–39.

Wilkins, A., & Blank, H. (1986). Child care: Strategies to move the issue forward. *Young Children, 42*(1), 68–72.

Zigler, E., & Finn, M. (1981). From problem to solution: Changing public policy as it affects children and families. *Young Children, 36*(4), 31–32, 55–59.

Chapter 5

Increasing Our Numbers and Building Our Strength

I t is not enough for a few people to advocate. Part of becoming an advocate is sharing our experiences with others. Strength and power will only happen when we increase our numbers and our effectiveness.

Each of us needs to encourage others to become advocates. When we send the message that early childhood advocacy is important, we legitimize it as an integral part of our training and help others see how to integrate it into their professional responsibilities. We encourage more people to speak out. As Anne Hunt (1988), an advocate in Tennessee, points out,

> [We] must give public policy activities as much emphasis as we do [any other aspect of] professional training. . . .
> Training and experience are giving us information and confidence. . . . We are feeling support, and on occasion, even power as we unite our efforts. . . . [We] are becoming a network of child advocates . . . evolving from a solo to a chorus—a chorus that blends many voices in harmony but retains the timbre and flavor of each. (p. 26)

The movement on behalf of children, families, and the early childhood profession is building, one person at a time. Through workshops and courses, meetings and contacts, we are encouraging others to join with us.

A supportive advocacy leader, like a good teacher, recognizes the importance of building personal relationships with the people she or he is guiding. Our effectiveness as advocates is not confined to our own ability to cause change. As leaders, we relate to others in ways that help them see that they too can make things happen. We build confidence. We enable emerging advocates to grow into their own role. We serve as models for taking action and speaking out on issues.

Fostering a belief in change

Too often people do not speak out because they think that their actions will not make a difference or that change is impossible. Institutional change is often slow. The problems that early childhood educators face are complex. Many people already put in long hours and receive low salaries for their work. But we must try not to feel overwhelmed by the time and energy it takes to move an issue forward.

It is not always easy to motivate people, to convince them that their actions can effect change. Sometimes we ask people to write letters to legislators, and the bills do not pass. Or we ask people to use developmentally appropriate teaching practices, and they face resistance from parents and administrators. We ask people to speak out to the business community, and they may encounter a lack of interest for investing private money in long-term solutions.

These realities should not force us to give up. Instead, we should reach out and support each other. We can maintain our enthusiasm and continue to foster a belief in change. We can support even small advocacy efforts by showing appreciation for individual and group contributions and by highlighting their successes along the way. We can join forces and overcome our differences to build a stronger voice for change.

Building confidence and skills

Many people lack the confidence to speak out. They resist taking action because they do not believe in their own power to effect change, or they feel that they may not have sufficient knowledge of how our government and other institutions operate.

Early childhood advocates can help overcome these barriers. We can:

1. Promote a positive professional self-concept within the field. We are experts in early childhood education. We have a wealth of information to share.

2. Stress that decision makers need to hear from us to better understand the issues. Although they may be in influential positions, they don't have all the answers. They need our expertise.

3. Provide the tools to help others get involved. Help others understand how policy is made, how institutions work, and how to influence decisions. When training others, demonstrate good teaching practices. Present information in a way that is clearly understood. Speaking "over people's heads" only adds confusion and undermines our effort to recruit more advocates.

4. Define the issues clearly and provide concrete suggestions for action when asking others to speak out. Once people see that the first step is not so difficult, they will probably be willing to take another one.

5. Be available to answer questions, guide people, and serve as an advisor or mentor to emerging advocates. First-time advocates may be intimidated when they speak out, especially if their views are met with opposition. When someone is there to share and listen to their concerns, or to clarify issues, it provides the encouragement to go forward (see "Advocates in Action," p. 86).

Allowing people to grow into the advocacy role

Developing any new skill takes time. When we reach out to new advocates, we need to recognize that they may have time constraints. In addition, some people have special areas of interest. We must allow people to take on the jobs that they are most comfortable doing. Some will be speakers, others writers, or planners, or researchers, or envelope stuffers. Each role is valuable and each is important.

Most of our advocacy efforts are done by volunteers, so we must help people to become more aware of the issues, to develop relationships with others involved, and to see that their contribution makes a difference.

Advocates in Action

California AEYC trains new leaders

The California AEYC has developed a training project called "Leadership Development in Public Policy." This project grew out of the need to support new leadership involvement in public policy and advocacy activities. In conceptualizing this effort, the existing leadership chose to design a program that would inspire others to action and would develop the skills necessary to effect change.

A subcommittee of the State Public Policy Committee developed the idea and presented it to the board. The plan recommended developing an advocacy curriculum that included objectives, student materials, and supplemental materials; and providing training using this curriculum to a representative from each of the state's Affiliate Groups. (The largest Affiliate in the state was allowed two representatives.)

Once the board passed the plan, they hired as a consultant a university professor who had been teaching a course on advocacy to write the curriculum. Affiliate members then made nominations for the "intern" positions. Interns were selected based on a review of qualifications, interest, and a personal interview by a committee of the state board.

The training program lasts one year and runs from January to October. Interns meet every other month in different areas of the state and twice in the state capital. The local Affiliate in that area is responsible for housing and accommodations.

During the first wave of interns, the state board paid for the travel of the interns; however, the responsibility for these costs is now being shared with Affiliates and individuals.

During these bimonthly sessions, interns meet for a full weekend program of training. Assignments include projects such as researching and analyzing local issues, contacting local officials and state representatives, preparing testimony, and other special projects. For example, two interns prepared a slide/tape show on the legislative process to be used at advocacy workshops.

In this first phase, the project has successfully trained a new cadre of early childhood advocates who have moved on to assume leadership roles in public policy for their Affiliate Groups. The dream of a few dedicated leaders has grown into a network of trained, committed advocates, working across the state to improve early childhood programs serving young children and their families.

Based on a telephone interview with Nancy Noble, January 1988

Serving as a model advocate

We must be willing to speak out, to stand up, and to model the kinds of actions we want others to take. People learn how to be advocates by watching others at work. We all probably recall people who inspired us at different points in our professional lives to become involved in working for change (Whitebook & Ginsburg, 1984).

Our willingness to stand up and speak out on early childhood issues demonstrates to our colleagues that they are not alone in their concerns. It sets an example to others that we have an important message to share. Together we can make a difference for young children, families, and the early childhood profession.

References

Hunt, A. (1988). From solo to chorus: Child advocacy in Tennessee. *Dimensions,* *16*(4), 23–26.

Whitebook, M., & Ginsburg, G. (Eds.). (1984). *Just working with kids: Preparing early childhood teachers to advocate for themselves and others.* Berkeley, CA: Child Care Employee Project.

Figure A.1
Structure of the U.S. Congress

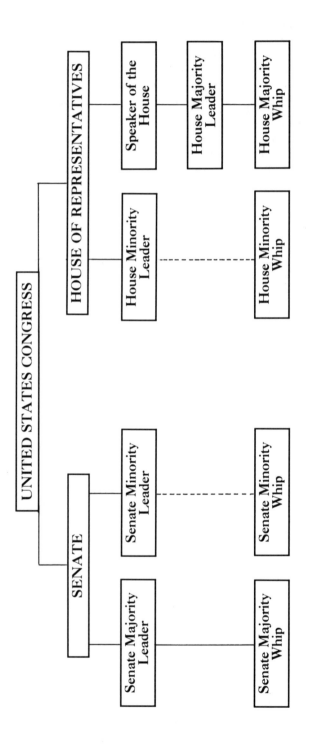

From *Understanding Congress* by Washington Monitor, 1982, Washington, DC: Author. Copyright 1982 by Washington Monitor. Reprinted by permission.

Appendix A

Structure of the U.S. Congress and the Path of Legislation

A dvocates interested in federal legislation need to know how the U.S. Congress works. The following should help give you a better understanding of the legislative process.

Structure of the U.S. Congress

The U.S. Congress is comprised of two houses, the *House of Representatives* and the *Senate*. There are 435 representatives (one for each congressional district) and 100 senators (two from each state). Members of the House are elected every 2 years; senators are elected for 6-year terms—one-third of them are up for election every 2 years. Each Congress sits for two sessions. For example, 1988 was the 100th Congress, second session.

In both the House and Senate, designated leaders set congressional priorities, establish timetables for legislative action, formulate strategies for passage (or defeat) of legislation, and encourage party unity (see Figure A.1, p. 88).

Standing committees deal with the many issues brought before Congress (see Figure A.2, p. 90). Each committee has a specific purpose. In addition, the House and Senate each have *select committees* that focus on short-term issues. Select committees generally do not have the power to enact legislation. Their purpose is to investigate issues and educate the public about special needs. *Joint committees* are formed with membership from both houses.

Figure A.2
Standing Committees of the U.S. Congress

House Standing Committees

Agriculture
Appropriations
Armed Services
Banking, Finance and Urban Affairs
Budget
District of Columbia
Education and Labor
Energy and Commerce
Foreign Affairs
Government Operations
House Administration
Interior and Insular Affairs
Judiciary
Merchant Marine and Fisheries
Natural Resources
Post Office and Civil Service
Public Works and Transportation
Rules
Science, Space and Technology
Small Business
Standards of Official Conduct
Veterans' Affairs
Ways and Means

Senate Standing Committees

Agriculture, Nutrition and Forestry
Appropriations
Armed Services
Banking, Housing and Urban Affairs
Budget
Commerce, Science and Transportation
Energy and Natural Resources
Environment and Public Works
Finance
Foreign Relations
Governmental Affairs
Indian Affairs
Judiciary
Labor and Human Resources
Rules and Administration
Small Business
Veterans' Affairs

Three distinct legislative processes take place in the U.S. Congress. The *budget process* is a series of actions by budget committees from both houses that leads to congressional approval of general spending targets for the upcoming year. The budget sets the outer spending limits for decision makers. The *authorization process* creates, amends, or renews programs through bills that define the content of programs. The *appropriation process* sets the actual funding of programs (Children's Defense Fund, 1980).

These three processes have corresponding committee structures in Congress. Both the Senate and the House have *budget committees* to set spending targets and *appropriations committees* to establish how much will actually be spent on a given program. In both the Senate and the House, specific committees authorize legislation in particular areas. Legislation affecting children falls under several different committees and subcommittees (see Figure A.3, p. 92).

Members of Congress generally request committee assignments based on their own, and their constituents', interests. Representatives usually serve on two or three committees, and senators on three or four. Find out on which committees your representative and senators serve so you can contact them when important legislation is pending in their committees.

The path of legislation

Most legislation follows a specific path, from the generation of an idea to the passage of a bill and executive action (see Figure A.4, p. 93). Although the process usually is lengthy, advocates must be prepared to mobilize on short notice, just in case something moves quickly.

Ideas for bills originate from various sources: legislators and their staff, constituents, interest groups, the executive branch, or judicial decisions. Once an idea surfaces and a bill is drafted, it will usually follow the path described here (adapted from Oakes, 1987).

Introduction and sponsorship

Any House or Senate member can introduce or cosponsor legislation. Often a representative and a senator offer similar proposals, called companion bills, that may be acted on simultaneously or at different times. Although some legislation may originate in the executive branch, only legislators can introduce a bill. Proposals often are introduced by the committee or subcommittee chair who has jurisdiction over the matter.

Figure A.3
Congressional Committees That Work on Children's Issues

Appropriations (House and Senate)—Item-by-item decisions on how much money to spend for each federal program program each year.

Budget (House and Senate)—Drafting and approving a congressional budget, which sets general spending targets for the coming year.

Education and Labor (House)—Authorization and oversight for education and labor programs, including Head Start, Title 1, Child Abuse Prevention and Treatment, and many others.

Energy and Commerce (House)—Authorization and oversight for Medicaid and a number of other important health programs.

Finance (Senate)—Authorization and oversight for all tax and revenue measures and a broad range of important children's programs, including AFDC, Title XX, SSI, Child Support, and Medicaid.

Ways and Means (House)—Authorization and oversight for a number of important children's programs, including Title XX, AFDC, and SSI.

Labor and Human Resources (Senate)—Authorization and oversight for a number of education, labor, and social programs, including Head Start, Title 1, and Child Abuse Prevention and Treatment.

Select Committee on Children, Youth and Families (House)—Study and review of problems of children, youth, and families and the development of policies that would encourage the coordination of both governmental and private programs designed to address these problems.

From *Lobby Day 1988* by the Children's Defense Fund, March 1988, unpublished document. Reprinted with permission.

Figure A.4
Typical Path of Legislation

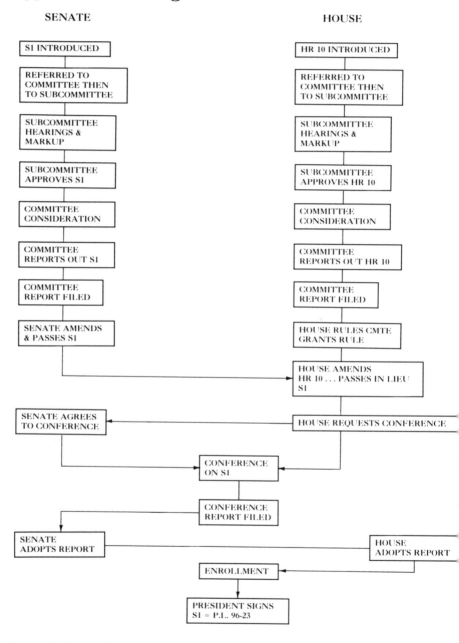

SENATE   HOUSE

SENATE	HOUSE
S1 INTRODUCED	HR 10 INTRODUCED
REFERRED TO COMMITTEE THEN TO SUBCOMMITTEE	REFERRED TO COMMITTEE THEN TO SUBCOMMITTEE
SUBCOMMITTEE HEARINGS & MARKUP	SUBCOMMITTEE HEARINGS & MARKUP
SUBCOMMITTEE APPROVES S1	SUBCOMMITTEE APPROVES HR 10
COMMITTEE CONSIDERATION	COMMITTEE CONSIDERATION
COMMITTEE REPORTS OUT S1	COMMITTEE REPORTS OUT HR 10
COMMITTEE REPORT FILED	COMMITTEE REPORT FILED
SENATE AMENDS & PASSES S1	HOUSE RULES CMTE GRANTS RULE

HOUSE AMENDS HR 10 ... PASSES IN LIEU S1

SENATE AGREES TO CONFERENCE ← HOUSE REQUESTS CONFERENCE

CONFERENCE ON S1

CONFERENCE REPORT FILED

SENATE ADOPTS REPORT   HOUSE ADOPTS REPORT

ENROLLMENT

PRESIDENT SIGNS S1 = P.L. 96-23

From *Understanding Congress* by Washington Monitor, 1982, Washington, DC: Author. Copyright 1982 by Washington Monitor. Reprinted by permission.

All bills are assigned numbers. In the House, these numbers are H.R. _____, and in the Senate they are S. _____.

To obtain copies of bills, contact your legislators. You can also get a single copy by writing to the Document Room of the House or Senate (see Figure A.5, below).

If you support a bill, you will want to urge your legislator to cosponsor it. The number and type of cosponsors often indicate the level of support for a bill. Generating a large number of cosponsors from both parties prior to introduction of the bill is often critical. Cosponsors can continue to sign on to the bill after it is introduced.

Figure A.5
Congressional Information

For telephone numbers of any office in the Capitol, House, and Senate, contact the Capitol switchboard, 202-224-3121. For single copies of bills, contact:

The House Document Room
Annex 2, Room B18
2nd and D Sts., S.W.
Washington, DC 20515

The Senate Document Room
Hart Senate Office Building
Room B 04
2nd St. and Constitution Ave., N.E.
Washington, DC 20510

Committee referral and consideration

After the bill is introduced, the usual first step is to refer it to a subcommittee of the most pertinent committee. Some bills may include topics that fall under the jurisdiction of different committees and therefore are referred to multiple committees.

The subcommittee holds hearings where witnesses testify. After hearings are completed, the subcommittee meets again to *mark up* the bill (to review it and make any changes). If a majority of the subcommittee members approve the bill, it is favorably reported to the full committee for further consideration. The full committee often repeats the process of holding hearings and a markup to prepare the bill for floor action.

Many measures are ignored, and thus killed, in committee. More than 10,000 bills and resolutions are introduced during each Congress, but only about 5% become law. Committees usually decide the fate of a bill, so it is essential that advocates voice support or opposition to bills with the committee chair (who decides which topics/issues/bills will be heard) and committee members.

Floor action

Committees refer bills to the full house. Discussion and a vote can be completed quickly or can be prolonged. A bill can be voted on by a voice vote, a roll call (recorded) vote, or, if there are no objections, by unanimous consent.

To voice support for or opposition to a bill, advocates must keep informed (through alerts or a telephone tree) about when a bill is scheduled to be voted upon.

Conference consideration

Companion bills may be similar when they are introduced, but differences usually emerge in markup. After both the House and Senate pass a bill, the measure is sent to a conference committee, composed of members from the relevant committees of both bodies, who iron out differences between the two versions. The resulting compromise, called a *conference report*, must then be passed, without amendments, by the full House and Senate before the bill can become a law.

Executive action

The approved conference report is next sent to the White House for the presidential signature (or veto). The President can veto a bill in two ways: (1) by sending a *veto message* to Congress outlining the offending provision(s), or (2) if Congress has adjourned, by taking no action on the bill within 10 days (excluding Sundays) after the measure reaches the President's desk (called a *pocket veto*).

Advocates should voice their support for or opposition to a bill with the White House before the President acts. Once again, it is important for you to stay well informed of the bill's progress so you can respond in a timely manner.

After a bill becomes law, the agency within the executive branch responsible for implementing and enforcing the law begins to draft regulations that specify how the law will be executed at the federal, state, and local levels. You can continue your advocacy by monitoring and participating in these administrative decisions.

Key Terms in the Legislative Process

Appropriation: A legislative process whereby House and Senate Appropriations Committees set actual spending levels for federal programs each year, within the limits set by authorization legislation and budget resolutions. Federal programs and agencies are grouped into 13 annual appropriations bills to be passed and signed by the President before the beginning of each fiscal year (October 1).

Authorization: A legislative process whereby the "authorizing committees" in each house of Congress establish, continue, or change federal programs under their jurisdiction. "Authorization legislation" sets spending ceilings for programs, usually for a period of several years, and determines the basic requirements guiding program operation. Congressional rules require that programs be properly "authorized" before actual funds may be appropriated for them.

Budget Resolution: Legislation, in the form of a concurrent resolution, that establishes general spending and revenue guidelines for the entire federal government each year. The President's proposed budget makes spending and revenue recommendations. Then Congress considers these recommendations and adopts a Concurrent Budget Resolution that finally sets the government's spending and revenue limits in general categories called *functions*. The Concurrent Budget Resolution must be adopted by both houses of Congress but does not require the President's signature.

Continuing Resolution: Legislation that continues funding for federal programs for which Congress has not completed regular annual legislation by the beginning of the fiscal year. Continuing Resolutions are a form of stop-gap, often omnibus appropriations legislation. A Continuing Resolution must be passed by both houses of Congress and signed by the President.

Discretionary Programs: Federal programs, other than entitlements, for which each year's amount of spending is set at the
"discretion" of the Appropriations Committees, within upper
limits established by the authorizing legislation and the budget
resolution. Many programs serving poor children and families,
including Head Start, the Maternal and Child Health Block
Grant, Immunizations, Child Welfare Services, Job Corps, and
the Title 1 program for education of the disadvantaged, are
discretionary programs.

Entitlement Programs: Federal programs, such as Medicaid, Aid to
Families with Dependent Children (AFDC), Food Stamps, and
Social Security, which are available to all persons who meet their
eligibility requirements. Means-tested entitlements are provided
to those eligible on the basis of income or "means," while non-
means-tested entitlements have no income test. Funding for
entitlement programs is contained in annual appropriations
legislation, but the amount of such funding is set according to
the level of benefits to be provided and the number of eligible
persons "entitled" to receive them. Key decisions regarding
eligibility and benefit levels are made by the authorizing committees.

Reconciliation: Legislation to implement the spending and revenue
limits in the Concurrent Budget Resolution, including any actual
program changes, tax changes, or spending changes necessary to
achieve required budget savings.

From *A Children's Defense Budget FY89* (pp. 306–307) by Children's
Defense Fund, 1988, Washington, DC: Author. Copyright 1988 by the
Children's Defense Fund. Reprinted by permission.

References

Children's Defense Fund. (1980). *Children and the federal budget: How to influence
the budget process.* Washington, DC: Author.
Oakes, M. (Ed.). (1987). *Your legislative guide to child advocacy.* Washington, DC:
National PTA Office of Governmental Relations.

Appendix B

The Executive Branch

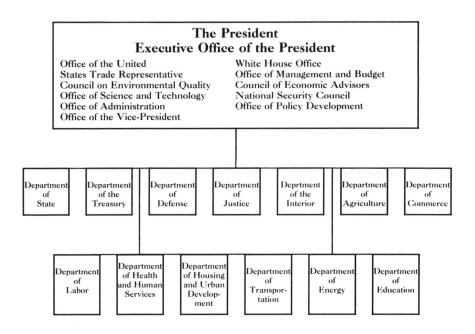

The President
Executive Office of the President

Office of the United States Trade Representative	White House Office
Council on Environmental Quality	Office of Management and Budget
Office of Science and Technology	Council of Economic Advisors
Office of Administration	National Security Council
Office of the Vice-President	Office of Policy Development

Department of State

Department of the Treasury

Department of Defense

Department of Justice

Deprtment of the Interior

Department of Agriculture

Department of Commerce

Department of Labor

Department of Health and Human Services

Department of Housing and Urban Development

Department of Transportation

Department of Energy

Department of Education

From *You and Your National Government* (p. 21) by League of Women Voters Education Fund, 1985, Washington, DC: Author. Copyright 1985 by the League of Women Voters Education Fund. Reprinted by permission.

Appendix C

Information To Share With Decision Makers

S tories and information from your own community or program are a good way to build awareness of early childhood issues. Every day you see firsthand the issues that face children and their families—so share what you know with the people who need to know!

Here are a few questions to get you started in your thinking.

When you talk about your community

- Are there enough child care and other preschool programs? Family day care homes? Infant programs? School-age programs? (Use waiting lists as examples.)
- Is there enough child care subsidy money for low- and moderate-income families? (Compare the average cost of child care in your community with average wages. If you are a parent, give an example of how much of your income goes to child care.)
- Are there enough local training opportunities for early childhood program staff?
- What are the average salaries of the staff in programs for young children? How do these low salaries affect turnover? How do they affect the quality of the program?
- Does your community have a resource and referral system to offer information to parents, coordinate training, and recruit new providers?

- Are all programs in your community required to be licensed or registered? Do these standards provide adequate protection to children? Do they promote developmental programs?
- How does the business community support programs for young children?
- What are the certification standards for teachers who work with children from birth through age 8?

When you talk about your program

- How many children do you serve and what are their ages?
- What program activities do you provide? Why are they important to children? What could be improved?
- What type of families do you serve? How are they involved in the program?
- How much do parents pay? Is it difficult for some parents to pay this amount?
- How long is your waiting list?
- What other services have parents requested or do they need?
- What are parents' reactions to your program? If you write to or visit the decision maker, you might include a one-page summary of parents' comments. When a decision maker visits your program, make sure parents are involved.
- What training and experiences do your staff have? What training would enable them to do their jobs better?
- How do they work with children and their parents?
- What is the salary range? What benefits are provided?
- What is the turnover and/or vacancy rate of staff?
- How difficult is it to find reliable substitutes?
- Where do the funds for your program come from? What budget constraints do you face? Provide a copy of NAEYC's "Where Your Child Care Dollars Go."
- How do you link with other community resources? What are the gaps in family services?
- What administrative problems do you face (transportation, training, recruitment, other)?

When you talk about the profession

- If you work in resource and referral: What types of services do you provide? What types of phone calls do you receive? What kinds of services appear to be needed?
- If you work in a college or university: Why is training important? Which students are choosing to enter the field? What is the scope of training you provide? What job opportunities are available for graduates?

Appendix D
Lobbying for Non Profits

This is a simplified guide for tax-exempt groups whose advocacy by members or clients is part of their program. It is based on federal laws and regulations. Check your own state's laws also; some places have no restrictions on lobbying by charitable organizations. Others require registration of all those who lobby frequently. Federally funded programs must also consider the additional limitation explained toward the end of this guide. For more detailed information about federal tax and program requirements, see the Children's Defense Fund's publication, *Lobbying and Political Activity for Non-Profits*.

I. Tax-exempt, private, nonprofit organizations can lobby Congress and state legislatures.

Within reasonable limits you can
- Write to your representative on organization letterhead;
- Call long distance to the Capitol at agency expense;
- Take a carload of people to the Capitol and get mileage paid by the agency; and
- Organize a letter-writing or phone campaign for a bill.

The limits are
- For small agencies, not more than 15% to 20% of the agency's total activities measured in dollars if the IRS is informed beforehand, 5% if not (consult before trying to push the limits);
- The lobbying activities must fall within the organization's general "charitable" or "civic" purposes; and
- Be able to show that no employees or clients were coerced into lobbying.

Under the IRS's rules, these things aren't even considered lobbying; you are permitted to

- Inform your members (not the general public) of legislative issues critical to the goals of the agency and take positions on them (but telling people to write to Congress would still be considered lobbying);
- Research and conduct nonpartisan analyses of legislation and state your position on such issues, as long as you give both sides so that people can draw reasonable conclusions;
- Invite legislators (or their staff) to visit your program to learn about your work or to explain what is going on with legislation;
- Attend workshops on how to lobby, generally; and
- Respond to official requests by legislative bodies.

Some things you can do as a private citizen are

- Work on legislative issues during lunch hours or after work. This does not count as agency lobbying. In public you should convey that you are speaking as a private citizen, although based partly on your experience with the agency;
- Put bumper stickers on your personal car, even if it is used in business; and
- Participate in other related groups that actively discuss politics and issues and that lobby in that group's name.

What happens if the agency breaks the rules:

- IRS can do an audit of your agency to see if you are spending a substantial portion of your funds on lobbying activities.
- If they substantiate such overspending, and your agency's limit is 5%, they can rescind your tax-exempt status.
- If they substantiate such overspending, and your agency's limit is 15 to 20%, they can levy a 25% tax on the money spent above the limit.
- If they determine that your agency has exceeded the limit by a substantial amount for four years, IRS can rescind your tax-exempt status. Then, contributions to your agency would no longer be tax-deductible.

II. Restrictions on the use of federal funds

For nonprofits who receive federal funds, these are in addition to the general rules.

These restrictions on lobbying apply to federally funded grants or contracts entered into after May 29, 1984.

You still can

- Lobby *local,* but not *state,* governmental bodies, using agency resources;
- Do nonpartisan analysis and education on issues, including inviting people to inform you on legislation, so long as it is not done in "support of" or knowing preparation for a lobbying effort;
- Use your own time to lobby your congressman or congresswoman as a private citizen if you use agency funds to fly to Washington to a legitimate program-related function; and
- Attempt to influence federal, state, or local *administrative* agency policies and regulations.

The limits are

- No use of your agency or its resources for direct lobbying of Congress or state legislators either on pending bills or to get bills introduced; and
- No exhorting of others to lobby Congress or a state legislator on pending bills or to get bills introduced.

The same restrictions apply to resources that are considered as a match for federal funds.

Penalties:

- If caught lobbying, there may be an audit exception (e.g., if you write a letter, the exception would be for the cost of the letter and would have to be repaid).
- If your lobbying violation is serious, you could get your funds cut or your grant eliminated.
- You should be aware that OMB's [the Office of Management and Budget's] rules require all federal agencies that administer grants or contracts to set up procedures for advance resolution (in consultation with OMB) of questions or disagreements which programs might have about whether or not the rules apply to their work. Once a determination has been made, it will be binding in any later administrative proceedings (e.g., an audit). However, this will not prevent the program from challenging the funding agency's determination in court, if it still disagrees.

From *Lobby Day 1988* by the Children's Defense Fund, March 1988, unpublished document. Reprinted by permission.

Appendix E

Guidelines for Developing Legislation Creating or Expanding Programs for Young Children

A position statement of the National Association for the Education of Young Children

Introduction

More and more states are showing interest in providing funds to create or expand early childhood programs. A growing number of states have initiated publicly funded early childhood programs in recent years, and other states are considering legislation to establish such programs. Such interest is well founded. Early childhood programs can be of central importance to policies for improving education, reforming welfare policy, or stimulating economic development in a state.

From the perspective of education, legislators and citizens wish to improve schools. A number of national reports have been released documenting current problems with our educational system and suggesting strategies for change. Early childhood programs are frequently among the prescriptive measures suggested, and with good reason. Research has clearly documented the beneficial effects of high quality early childhood programs, particularly for children deemed vulnerable for later school failure. Children attending high quality early childhood programs have been found to have greater self-confidence and self-esteem, to be more likely to complete high school and continue their education, and to be less likely to be placed in remedial classes. (For an overview of these and other findings, see Howes, 1986.) Moreover, high quality early childhood programs are cost-effective. In one program, it was estimated that every $1 invested led to a return of $4.75 in savings as a result of lower special education costs, lower welfare costs, and higher worker productivity as the children matured (Weikart, 1983).

From the perspective of welfare and job training for parents, provisions for early childhood programs remove a major stumbling block for parental employment, thus reducing welfare costs and promoting self-sufficiency over time. High quality child care arrangements that meet families' needs can also make it easier for parents to stay on the job. Research clearly shows the links between parents' lower productivity and missed days of work and unsatisfactory child care arrangements. Finally, the provision of early childhood programs can stimulate economic development. Employers who provide financial support to early childhood programs and support services are quick to report positive results—a competitive edge in recruiting skilled employees and improved job performance and productivity because of lower absenteeism, reduced turnover, and less anxiety by parents.

No matter what the incentive for creating or expanding early childhood programs—whether to improve education, reduce welfare rolls, or stimulate economic development—there are a number of common denominators to consider as programs are designed and implemented. Problems may arise if programs are developed with consideration to only one perspective. For example, a program designed to provide enrichment experiences for children at risk for school failure may exacerbate parents' problems of locating or retaining employment if the program is scheduled on a part-day basis with no consideration given to parents' need to provide supplemental care during the full workday. This is particularly critical given the fact that children deemed at risk are likely to have parents who would benefit from assistance to obtain and retain employment.

Similarly, early childhood programs designed strictly from the perspective of welfare reform or economic development must not overlook the importance of addressing each child's right to a sound program that provides appropriate educational and social experiences geared to the age of the child. Programs designed *only* to meet parents' need to provide for their children while they work can lead to negative outcomes for children. High quality programs that meet children's developmental needs result in a wiser investment of public dollars because of their long-term cost effectiveness.

The National Association for the Education of Young Children (NAEYC) welcomes current public interest in early childhood programs. For the investment of public dollars to be most effective, high quality programs must be provided. The NAEYC suggests the following questions be used as yardsticks when legislation to create new or expand existing programs for young children and their families is considered, to assure that high quality programs for young children and their families are implemented.

Guidelines

Provision of program standards to assure quality programs

1. Does the legislation spell out a process for developing and effectively implementing standards that ensure the safety and well-being of the children served, while promoting their healthy development?

    a. If the process is the state's licensing system, does the licensing office have adequate staffing to handle the expansion and are the standards adequate to accomplish the purposes of the legislation?

    b. If the process is *not* licensing because programs may be delivered primarily through public agencies, does the legislation include wording to assure that the new programs will be at least equal to or surpass in quality programs licensed by the state?

    c. When standards are developed, does the legislation assure that program standards address each of the following areas:
- staff qualifications,
- parent role,
- group size and staff-child ratios,
- discipline, and
- developmentally appropriate practice?

    d. Does the legislation assure that there will be a system for implementing the standards that includes monitoring and inspections?

2. Does the legislation require that an advisory committee, composed in part of members with early childhood expertise, approve the program standards once developed?

3. Does the legislation assure that the appropriate use of evaluation instruments and procedures is addressed within the program standards?

    a. Are decisions regarding enrollment, retention, and placement in special classes based primarily on observations by parents and qualified professionals, rather than on a single test score?

    b. Is developmental assessment of children's progress and achievement used to plan curriculum, identify children with special needs, communicate with parents, and evaluate the program's effectiveness?

Parental access and involvement

1. Does the legislation provide opportunities for families to make informed choices concerning the program they want for their child? (e.g., Can parents choose either home-based child care or a center-based program? Can parents choose a school near their work site as well as near their home?)

2. Does the legislation assure the establishment of close ties between program staff and children's families?

    a. Are staff required to inform parents or guardians of the program's philosophy and operating procedures?

    b. Are parents provided with ongoing opportunities to discuss their children's needs and progress with program staff?

    c. Are parent representatives included as members of pertinent advisory groups?

    d. Do parents have unrestricted access to the program facility?

3. Does the legislation make provision for a variety of family needs, including those of working families, by allowing the funding of full-day programs (covering the average parent's working day) as well as part-day programs?

Eligibility for service

1. Is the long-term goal of the legislation to provide services to all children? If the legislation or available resources restrict service provision, is the target group the most needy?

2. Will the legislation extend eligibility to previously unserved or underserved groups (e.g., teenage parents, families who would be poor without subsidized early childhood programs)?

3. Does the legislation facilitate a socioeconomic mix of children in programs through the use of such mechanisms as sliding fee scales and other funding sources?

Linkages and coordination

1. Does the legislation provide the administering agency flexibility to fund a variety of public and private community agencies that demonstrate the ability to provide high quality early childhood services?

2. Does the legislation encourage or require programs to make linkages with other funding sources in order to serve more children (e.g., in-kind contributions, parent fees, coordinative agreements, and matching funds from private and public sources)?

3. Does the legislation encourage collaboration among the various agencies whose programs affect young children and their families (e.g., legislative creation of an Interagency Committee or other such mechanism to assure coordination of service provision for young children and their families)?

4. Does the legislation contribute to the overall provision of services for young children and avoid duplicating existing public or private programs?

Provision of professional expertise

1. Does the legislation require programs to employ persons with early childhood professional expertise at all stages of development and implementation and does it assure adequate compensation for those who work with young children?

2. Are advisory groups that include members of the early childhood profession as well as parent and community representatives legislatively created at both the state and program level?

3. Are the staff responsible for implementation in the administering agency and at the program level required to have specialized training related to the age of children served and work experience with this age group?

Funding

1. Will the legislation provide adequate funds per child to assure program quality and permit adequate compensation for staff?

2. Are funds tied to continued effort to meet standards?

3. Will the legislation provide for increased funding reflective of the cost of living?

Adopted November 1986

References

Howes, C. (1986). *Keeping current in child care research: An annotated bibliography.* Washington, DC: NAEYC.

Weikart, D.P. (1983). Testimony before the U.S. House of Representatives Select Committee on Children, Youth and Families. In *Prevention strategies for healthy babies and healthy children.* Hearing before the Select Committee on Children, Youth and Families, June 30, 1983. Washington, DC: U.S. Government Printing Office.

Appendix F

National Organizations

Administration for Children, Youth and Families (ACYF)
P.O. Box 1182
Washington, DC 20013
202-205-8347

The primary agency within the federal government with responsibility for serving children and families. The three major bureaus are The Children's Bureau, The Head Start Bureau, and the Family and Youth Services Bureau.

American Academy of Pediatrics
141 Northwest Point Blvd.
P.O. Box 927
Elk Grove, IL 60009-0627
800-433-9016

Provides information on health issues related to child care and young children.

American Association of University Women
1111 16th St., N.W.
Washington, DC 20036
202-785-7715

A membership organization of college and university graduates with branches in communities across the country. Many branches have strong legislative focus and interest in children's issues.

American Bar Association
The National Legal Resource Center for Child Advocacy and Protection
1800 M St., N.W., Suite 200 S.
Washington, DC 20036
202-331-2250

Provides training and technical assistance to the child welfare community and serves as a clearinghouse on child welfare issues.

American Federation of State, County and Municipal Employees— AFL-CIO
1625 L St., N.W.
Washington, DC 20036
202-429-1130

The largest AFL-CIO union, representing 1.4 million public employees. Materials include videotapes, booklets, and public opinion polls on child care.

American Public Welfare Association
810 First St., N.E., Suite 500
Washington, DC 20002
202-293-7550

The national organization representing state human service agencies and local welfare departments.

Association for Childhood Education International (ACEI)
11501 Georgia Ave., Suite 315
Wheaton, MD 20902
301-942-2443 or 800-423-3563

A membership organization whose purpose is to establish, promote, and maintain high standards and practice for childhood learning and growth. A wide range of publications available on education and child care issues. Journal published five times a year.

Association for Supervision and Curriculum Development (ASCD)
1250 N. Pitt St.
Alexandria, VA 22314-1453
703-549-9110

Membership organization focused on curriculum and supervision. Currently has a focus on early childhood education. Publication on public school early childhood programs available along with others on early childhood issues, and journal.

Association of Child Advocates
P.O. Box 5873
Cleveland, OH 44101-0873
216-881-2225 FAX

A national association of state-based child advocacy organizations. Provides an information systems network and technical assistance. Sponsors an annual conference on advocacy for children.

Association of Junior Leagues, Inc.
660 First Ave.
New York, NY 10016
212-683-1515

A membership organization with a history of concern and action in dealing with quality child care.

Center for Career Development in Early Care and Education
Wheelock College
200 The Riverway
Boston, MA 02215
617-734-5200, ext. 211

Center for Law and Social Policy
1616 P St., N.W., Suite 350
Washington, DC 20036
202-328-5140

A public-interest law firm; takes an active role in welfare reform.

Center for Public Advocacy Research
12 W. 37th St.
New York, NY 10018

Committed to identifying important policy concerns, conducting research, and advocating for sound policy

on issues affecting women, children, and youth. Reports on child care studies available on topics such as salaries and parents' concerns about policy.

Child Care Action Campaign
330 7th Ave., 7th Floor
New York, NY 10001
212-239-0138

A coalition of leaders from diverse organizations advocating for high-quality child care. Activities include education, information service, proposing possible solutions, and technical assistance to governmental offices. Publishes bimonthly newsletter.

The Child Care Law Center
22 Second St., Fifth Floor
San Francisco, CA 94105
415-495-5498

Extensive information and assistance in legal and business aspects of child care. Tracks and reports on such issues as religious exemptions to licensing, zoning family day care, the inclusion of child care in the land-use development process, and several other topics.

The Child Welfare League of America
440 First St., N.W., Suite 310
Washington, DC 20001
202-638-2952

A membership organization composed of people serving children and their families. Devoted to helping deprived, neglected, and abused children and families. Publishes a wide variety of material on advocacy and child care.

The Children's Defense Fund
25 E St., N.W.
Washington, DC 20001
202-628-8787 or 800-424-9602

Education about and advocacy for the needs of children, especially low-income, minority, and children with disabilities. Publications include a monthly newsletter, an annual analysis of the federal budget, and annual report on child care facts in the states.

The Children's Foundation
725 15th St., N.W., Suite 505
Washington, DC 20005
202-347-3300

Information and materials on home-based child care issues. Publishes the *Family Day Care Bulletin* and *Directory of Family Child Care Associations*. Also sponsors the National Family Child Care Advocacy Project and a resource clearinghouse.

Coalition of Labor Union Women
1126 16th St., N.W.
Washington, DC 20036
202-466-4610

A membership organization of female and male trade unionists interested in promoting working women's rights. Advocates for child care and family issues. Publications include "Bargaining for Child Care: A Union Parent's Guide."

Committee on Economic Development
477 Madison Ave.
New York, NY 10022
212-688-2063

A public policy research group whose membership includes mostly corporate executives. Report on *Children in Need* available.

Concerned Educators Allied for a Safe Environment (CEASE)
17 Gerry St.
Cambridge, MA 02138
617-864-0999

A national network of parents, teachers, and other advocates for young children working on peace and environmental issues. Newsletter and other publications available.

Council for Early Childhood Professional Recognition
1341 G St., N.W.
Washington, DC 20005
202-265-9090 or 800-424-4310

Credentials home-based child care providers, preschool and infant-toddler center-based caregivers, and home visitors. Bilingual specialization available.

Council for Exceptional Children Division for Early Childhood
1920 Association Dr.
Reston, VA 22901-1589
703-620-3660

Seeks to advance the education of exceptional children, both with disability and gifted. Serves as an information broker and produces numerous publications.

Council of State Governments
444 North Capitol St., N.W., Suite 401
Washington, DC 20001
202-624-5460

Publishes a wide variety of reports and studies on important issues facing states and state legislative structures.

Education Commission of the States
707 17th St., Suite 2700
Denver, CO 80202-3427
303-299-3600

An interstate compact that helps state leaders improve the quality of education in their states. Conducts policy research, surveys, and special studies; has an information clearinghouse; gives technical assistance to states. Reports include "Family Involvement in the Schools."

ERIC Clearinghouse on Elementary and Early Childhood Education (ERIC/EECE)
University of Illinois
805 W. Pennsylvania Ave.
Urbana, IL 61801-4877
217-333-1386

Publishes free newsletter on materials, publications, and events. Computer searches on any early childhood topic (ask your local librarian for more information).

Family Resource Coalition
200 S. Michigan Ave., Suite 1520
Chicago, IL 60604
312-341-0900

A national grassroots network of individuals and organizations promoting the development of prevention-oriented, community-based programs to strengthen families. Serves as a national clearinghouse; provides technical assistance, a wide variety of publications, and a newsletter three times a year.

Families and Work Institute
330 Seventh Ave.
New York, NY 10001
212-465-2044

Food Research Action Coalition (FRAC)
1875 Connecticut Ave., N.W.,
 Suite 540
Washington, DC 20009
202-986-2200

Works on issues of hunger and poverty in America. Wide range of publications including guide to state legislation on the operation of federal food programs.

High/Scope Educational Research Foundation
600 N. River St.
Ypsilanti, MI 48198-2898
313-485-2000

A research development and training center whose principal focus is early childhood education. Newsletter and a wide variety of publications.

Institute for Women's Policy Research
1400 20th St., N.W., Suite 104
Washington, DC 20036
202-785-5100

Conducts research that informs public policy debate on women's issues. Fact sheet and papers on child care wages.

League of Women Voters
1730 M St., N.W.
Washington, DC 20036
202-429-1965

A citizens' education and research organization with a wide variety of publications on becoming more politically effective.

National Association for the Education of Young Children (NAEYC)
1509 16th St., N.W.
Washington, DC 20036-1426
202-232-8777 or 800-424-2460
FAX 202-328-1846

The largest professional group of early childhood educators. Publishes the journal Young Children, brochures, posters, videotapes, and books. National, state, and local Affiliate Groups offer training opportunities. Other programs are the Information Service and the Week of the Young Child.

National Association for Family Child Care
1331A Pennsylvania Ave., N.W., #348
Washington, DC 20004
800-359-3817

Membership organization representing the needs and concerns of family day care providers, young children, parents, and child advocates.

National Association of Child Care Resource and Referral Agencies (NACCRRA)
1319 F St., N.W., Suite 606
Washington, DC 20004
202-393-5501

Promotes the development, maintenance, and expansion of quality child care resources and referral. Newsletter, bulletins, and other publications.

National Association of Counties
440 First St., N.W., 8th Floor
Washington, DC 20001
202-393-6226

Tracks issues facing counties—wide range of publications.

National Association of Early Childhood Specialists in State Departments of Education (NAECS/SDE)
(Call NAEYC for current address.)

A national association of early childhood specialists who work in state education agencies. Position statement available on kindergarten entry and placement.

National Association of Early Childhood Teacher Educators
338 Peik Hall
University of Minnesota
Minneapolis, MN 55455
612-625-4039

Membership organization focused on early childhood teacher education issues. Publishes a journal three times a year.

National Association of Elementary School Principals
1615 Duke St.
Alexandria, VA 22314
703-684-3345

Represents and reports on issues facing elementary school principals. Journal published five times a year with May issue focused on early childhood education.

National Association of State Boards of Education (NASBE)
1012 Cameron St.
Alexandria, VA 22314
703-684-4000

Tracks issues and publishes reports on early childhood education issues in the states.

National Black Child Development Institute
1023 15th St., N.W., Suite 600
Washington, DC 20005
202-387-1281

A membership organization that publishes a newsletter and policy reports relevant to issues facing Black

children. Publications include guidelines for establishing early childhood programs in public schools.

National Center for Early Childhood Workforce
733 15th St., N.W., Suite 800
Washington, DC 20005
202-737-7700
FAX 202-737-0370

A clearinghouse on child care employee issues, including salaries, status, and working conditions. Will provide technical assistance on conducting salary surveys. Publications on such topics as comparable worth/ job discrimination, personnel policies, salary surveys, and strategies to raise child care workers' salaries. Newsletter, by subscription.

National Coalition for Campus Child Care, Inc.
P.O. Box 413
Milwaukee, WI 53201

A membership organization that focuses on campus child care issues. Newsletter and other publications available.

National Commission on Working Women/Wider Opportunities for Women
1325 G St., N.W., Lower Level
Washington, DC 20005
202-737-5764

Focuses on the needs and concerns of the approximately 80% of women in the work force concentrated in low-paying, low-status jobs. Publications on child care employee issues.

National Committee for the Prevention of Child Abuse
332 S. Michigan Ave., Suite 1600
Chicago, IL 60604-4357
312-663-3520

Serves as a clearinghouse with a wide variety of publications on child abuse prevention.

National Conference of State Legislatures
444 N. Capitol St., N.W., Suite 515
Washington, DC 20001
202-624-5400

Serves the country's state lawmakers and their staffs. A wide variety of information on state legislatures and issues they face, including early childhood education.

National Council of Churches Ecumenical Child Care Network
475 Riverside Dr., Room 572
New York, NY 10115-0050
212-870-3342

Membership organization that serves church-housed child care programs. Newsletter and a variety of publications on child care.

National Council of Jewish Women
53 W. 23rd St.
New York, NY 10010
212-645-4048

A membership organization with sections nationwide. Has child study center that focuses on child care and family issues.

National Governors' Association
444 N. Capitol St., N.W., Suite 267
Washington, DC 20001
202-624-5300

The association of state governors, which focuses on shaping and implementation of national policy and leadership on state issues. A variety of publications on state issues including child care.

National Head Start Association
201 N. Union St., Suite 320
Alexandria, VA 22314
703-739-0875

The association of directors, parents, friends, and staff of Head Start. Quarterly newsletter.

National League of Cities
1301 Pennsylvania Ave., N.W.,
  6th Floor
Washington, DC 20004
202-626-3000

Focuses on issues facing U.S. cities. Publication available on children and family issues.

National Organization for Women (NOW) Legal Defense and Education Fund
1000 16th St., N.W., Suite 700
Washington, DC 20036
202-331-0066

Dedicated to achieving equal opportunities for women in the workplace, in schools, in the courts, and in the family. Publications on child care tax credit.

National PTA Office of Governmental Relations
2000 L St., N.W., Suite 600
Washington, DC 20036
202-331-1380

A membership organization representing parents in more than 26,000 schools, including preschools. Child care publications available.

National Urban League
1111 14th St., N.W., 6th Floor
Washington, DC 20005
202-898-1604

Social services and civil rights organization with local affiliates in 34 states. Sponsors national forums on various child care issues.

National Women's Law Center
1616 P St., N.W., Suite 100
Washington, DC 20036
202-328-5160

National legal association working on issues that affect women, especially low-income women. Several child care publications, including child care tax credit.

9–5 National Association of Working Women
614 Superior Ave., N.W., Suite 852
Cleveland, OH 44113
216-566-9308

Membership group for office workers. Child care, along with other working-family policies, is a strong group focus.

Parent Action
2 North Charles St., Suite 960
Baltimore, MD 21201
410-727-3687

Save the Children Child Care Support Center
1447 Peach Tree St., N.E., Suite 700
Atlanta, GA 30309-3030
404-885-1578

Sponsors yearly conference for home-based child care providers. Publications include a guide to home-based child care and audiovisual training resources.

School-Age Child Care Project
Wellesley College Center for Research on Women
106 Central St.
Wellesley, MA 02181-8259
617-283-2547

Clearinghouse on school-age child care issues; publishes newsletter and policy reports.

Society for Research in Child Development
5720 South Woodlawn Ave.
Chicago, IL 60637
312-702-7470

Focuses on child development research. Publishes newsletter, journal, and other information important to advocates.

Southern Association of Early Childhood (SAEC)
P.O. Box 56130, Brady Station
Little Rock, AR 72215
501-663-0353

A membership organization, with members in 13 southern states, committed to the welfare of children and families and the professionals who serve them. Journals, books, and position statements available.

United Way of America
701 North Fairfax St.
Alexandria, VA 22314-2045
703-836-7100

U.S. Department of Commerce—Bureau of the Census
Washington, DC 20233

Public Information Office
301-763-7662

Data User Services Division
301-763-4100

U.S. Department of Labor—Bureau of Labor Statistics
441 G St., N.W.
Washington, DC 20212
202-606-7828

Work/Family Directions, Inc.
930 Commonwealth Ave. W.
Boston, MA 02215-1274
617-278-4000

Offers a broad range of options and services to assist companies in adapting to the changing labor force. Provides a national resource and referral network for companies. Publications include compilation of state child care regulations.

Work and Family Information Center
The Conference Board
845 Third Ave.
New York, NY 10022
212-759-0900

Clearinghouse for information concerning interrelationship between work and family, and employer-supported child care, including resource and referral services, family day care satellites, and parent fee subsidies.

Zero to Three/National Center for Clinical Infant Programs
2000 14th St., N., Suite 380
Arlington, VA 22201
703-528-4300
703-528-6848 FAX

Publishes information and sponsors conferences on infant health and development. Newsletter published five times a year.

Appendix G

Resources for Early Childhood Advocates

T here are hundreds of new reports and publications currently available on a wide variety of important early childhood issues. Contact NAEYC's Public Affairs Office (202-328-2605 or 800-424-2460) and the Information Service (202-328-2603 or 800-424-2460) to obtain a list of publications on specific topics.

The following resources will be useful in helping you plan effective advocacy strategies.

The Children's Defense Fund (25 E St., N.W., Washington, DC 20001) publishes the following:

Child care: The time is now. (1987). Provides compelling arguments for child care, the effects of funding cuts, state child care standards, child care workers' salaries, and the rationale for the ABC bill.

Children and the federal budget: How to influence the budget process. (1980). Describes the federal budget process.

A children's defense budget: An analysis of the FY 19[ ] federal budget and children (published yearly). An indepth examination of federal policies and programs affecting children, youth, and families.

CDF's nonpartisan voting record of 19[ ] (updated regularly). Tracks positions by all members of the House and Senate on key votes for children and families.

It's time to stand up for your children. (1979). Designed for parents, this booklet can also be used to explain child advocacy to anyone interested in the topic. It answers questions such as, What is child advocacy? What do you do? What can you expect?

Shur, J.L., & Smith, P.V. (1980). *Where do you look? Whom do you ask? How do you know?* Information resources for child advocates.

118

State child care fact book (published yearly). Provides a review of state child care initiatives and a compilation of state child care funding statistics and state contacts.

League of Women Voters (1730 M St., N.W., Washington, DC 20036) publishes the following:

Anatomy of a hearing. (1972). To help citizens and groups present their causes effectively in public hearings.

Going to court in the public interest: A guide for community groups. (1983). Recent information on how to finance public interest litigation, including how to litigate on a small budget, how to find and work with a lawyer, and how the court system works.

Know your community. (1972). Guide to help citizens and organizations interested in change take a good look at the existing structure and function of their government.

Know your county. (1974). Outline for making a complete survey of the structure and functions of county government.

Know your schools. (1974). Outline to help citizens analyze their schools: organization, operation, financing, and education programs.

Tell it to Washington (updated biennially). Lists House and Senate members and major committee rosters of Congress. Provides tips on how to lobby more effectively.

National Association for the Education of Young Children (NAEYC) (1509 16th St., N.W., Washington, DC 20036-1426) publishes the following:

Employer-assisted child care resource guide (rev. ed.). (1988). Lists organizations, programs, contact people, and state and local initiatives.

Information kit on employer-assisted child care. (1986). Package of materials to be used when approaching businesses for support of child care.

National Center for Early Childhood Workforce (733 15th St., N.W., Suite 800, Washington, DC 20005) publishes the following:

Beyond "just working with kids": Preparing early childhood teachers to advocate for themselves and others. (1984). A curriculum guide for teaching advocacy, based on six concepts: the process of social change; social and economic organization of society; multicultural perspectives; the value and image of child care; the nature, economics, and organization of child care; and child care's link with other social services.

Friedman, J., Ginsburg, G., & Whitebook, M. (1984). *Managing the media maze: A resource guide for child care advocates.* Planning your approach and specific strategies to use the media.

Whitebook, M., Pemberton, C., Lombardi, J., Galinsky, E., Bellm, D., & Fillinger, G. (1988). *Raising salaries: Strategies that work.* Examples of successful advocacy efforts to raise salaries.

＊ ＊ ＊

American Public Welfare Association. (1988). *Public welfare directory, 1988–89: A resource guide to the human services.* American Public Welfare Association, 810 First St., N.E., Suite 500, Washington, DC 20002.

Compilation of important human service contacts, including local, county, and regional agencies; Washington, D.C. offices of each governor; state research and demonstration directors; and much more useful information for advocates.

Bing, S.R., & Richart, D.W. (1987). *Fairness is a kid's game: A background paper for child advocates.* Indianapolis: The Lilly Endowment, Inc. Available from Kentucky Youth Advocates, Inc., 2034 Frankfort Ave., Louisville, KY 40206.

Written for state-based advocacy organizations, this report is a particularly good reference for helping state and local advocacy groups decide their goals and strategies.

Child Care Action Campaign media kit. (1986). Child Care Action Campaign, 330 7th Ave., 7th Floor, New York, NY 10001.

Media kit to help state and local organizations and child care advocates learn how to tell their stories.

Child Welfare League of America. *CWLA Washington workbook for child advocates [ ]th Congress 19[ ]–19[ ]* (updated biennially). Child Welfare League of America, 440 First St., N.W., Suite 310, Washington, DC 20001.

Tips for working with Congress and a list (with pictures) of current members of Congress by state. Also included are the members of all congressional committees.

Freeman, M. (1986). *Called to act: Stories of child care advocacy in our churches.* National Council of Churches, 475 Riverside Dr., New York, NY 10115-0050.

This book provides principles of advocacy, as well as actual stories of child care advocates working in church groups.

Kelman, S. (1987). *Making public policy: A hopeful view of American government.* New York: Basic.

A detailed account of both the institutions and democratic practice in policymaking.

OMB Watch. (1987). *Through the coordination of power.* OMB Watch, 1731 Connecticut Ave., N.W., 4th Floor, Washington, DC 20009.

A guide to federal agency rule making for the layperson.

Pizzo, P. (1983). *Parent to parent.* Boston: Beacon Press. Looks at parents as activists and provides a wealth of examples of self-help and advocacy groups developed by parents.

About the Authors

Stacie G. Goffin, Ed.D., is currently senior specialist in early childhood education and policy at the Ewing Marion Kauffman Foundation in Kansas City, Missouri. Formerly, she was an early childhood faculty member at the University of Missouri—Kansas City. Prior to teaching at the college level, she worked in non-profit and public school programs, teaching young children with special needs. Her most recent publications include *Curriculum Models and Early Childhood Education: Appraising the Relationship,* published by Macmillan, and *Visions of Entitlement: The Care and Education of America's Children,* coedited with Mary Jensen and published by SUNY Press. Her forthcoming publication with David Day is entitled *New Perspectives in Early Childhood Teacher Education,* to be published by Teachers College Press.

Joan Lombardi, Ph.D., is an early childhood specialist from Alexandria, Virginia. After teaching and directing community-based early childhood programs, she worked at the national level with the Administration for Children, Youth and Families, and later as deputy director of the CDA National Credentialing Program. She has served as a consultant to the Head Start Bureau, as senior staff associate for the Early Childhood Task Force of the National Association of State Boards of Education, and as a representative of the Child Care Employee Project (now the National Center for Early Childhood Workforce) in Washington, D.C. At the state level she served as a consultant to the Children's Defense Fund Virginia Child Care Project and as public policy chair for the state and local AEYC Affiliates. She has also served as a member of the NAEYC Governing Board.

121

Information about NAEYC

NAEYC is . . .

. . . a membership-supported organization of people committed to fostering the growth and development of children from birth through age 8. Membership is open to all who share a desire to serve and act on behalf of the needs and rights of young children.

NAEYC provides . . .

. . . educational services and resources to adults who work with and for children, including

• *Young Children, the* journal for early childhood educators

• **Books, posters, brochures,** and **videos** to expand your knowledge and commitment to young children, with topics including infants, curriculum, research, discipline, teacher education, and parent involvement

• An **Annual Conference** that brings people from all over the country to share their expertise and advocate on behalf of children and families

• **Week of the Young Child** celebrations sponsored by NAEYC Affiliate Groups across the nation to call public attention to the needs and rights of children and families

• **Insurance plans** for individuals and programs

• **Public affairs information** for knowledgeable advocacy efforts at all levels of government and through the media

• The **National Academy of Early Childhood Programs,** a voluntary accreditation system for high-quality programs for children

• The **National Institute for Early Childhood Professional Development,** providing resources and services to improve professional preparation and development of early childhood educators

• The **Information Service,** a centralized source of information sharing, distribution, and collaboration

For free information about membership, publications, or other NAEYC services . . .

• call NAEYC at 202-232-8777 or 1-800-424-2460,

• or write to the National Association for the Education of Young Children, 1509 16th Street, N.W., Washington, DC 20036-1426.